D0065710

To

From

Date

YOU MATTER

Devotions & Prayers
for a
Teen Girl's Heart

Margot Starbuck

YOU MATTER

Devotions & Prayers
for a
Teen Girl's Heart

BARBOUR BOOKS
An Imprint of Barbour Publishing, Inc.

"Don't be afraid, I've redeemed you.
I've called your name. You're mine. . . .
That's how much you mean to me!
That's how much I love you!
I'd sell off the whole world to get you back,
trade the creation just for you."
ISAIAH 43:2–4 MSG

If you're like most girls, you have some great days and some more diffi-cult ones. You have days when you feel like you're on top of the world and you also have ones when it doesn't feel like anyone notices you or cares for you. And even with friends and family who love and support you, you need a solid anchor to ground you in what is most true about you and about God.

You Matter has been written to remind you how much God loves and values you. It contains 180 encouraging readings, Bible verses, and prayers, all of which end with takeaway faith-boosting statements you can carry with you throughout the day.

Because you matter, you can be grounded in God's big love for you every day. Because you matter, God wants to use you to touch the lives of those around you. And because you matter, God has a good future in store for you.

Today, and every day, you belong to God and He calls you by name.

I AM FEARFULLY AND WONDERFULLY MADE

For you created my inmost being; you knit me
together in my mother's womb. I praise you because
I am fearfully and wonderfully made; your works
are wonderful, I know that full well.

PSALM 139:13–14

When you're having a rough day, have you ever wondered about your worth? If a friend has blown you off or if it feels like no one cares about you, have you wondered whether your life even matters at all? A lot of girls have had thoughts like that. In the Psalms, we hear from a writer who knows where to find the answer to that question. This writer has prayerfully imagined the very early beginnings of her life, and she sees God knitting her together inside her mother's body. Isn't that a wild and beautiful image? Can you see God forming and perfecting you in the same way? You are immeasurably worthy because you are God's handiwork. You are precious to God, and you are infinitely loved.

God, I confess that I am not always feeling my worth
with the confidence of this psalmist! But I do trust
Your Word, and I believe that You made me,
You treasure me, and You love me. Amen.

BEARING THE HOLY IMAGE OF GOD

So God created mankind in his own image, in the image of
God he created them; male and female he created them.
GENESIS 1:27

When you look at your baby pictures, who do you resemble? Do you have your mom's smile? Does everyone say you look like your dad? If you're adopted, like me, your features might be a little glimpse into the ones from whom you came! For better or worse, people expect us to resemble the ones who "made" us. In the ancient Near East, it was believed that nations' kings were earthly representatives of a particular god. So to claim that every individual reflected the image of God was a *radical* notion! It won't be your eye color or hair texture that belie your roots though. It will be the undeniable dignity and worth you bear as someone who's been made in God's image.

Lord, You know there are days I struggle to believe
I am worthy. But Your Word teaches me that I am
valuable and precious and worthy because I bear
the holy imprint of Your image. Today, I hold
on to that assurance. Amen.

CALLED TO SERVE

Moses said, I will now turn aside and see this great sight,
why the bush is not burned. And when the Lord saw that he
turned aside to see, God called to him out of the midst of
the bush and said, Moses, Moses! And he said, Here am I.
EXODUS 3:3–4 AMPC

Have you ever seen the classic animated version, *Prince of Egypt*? God appears to Moses in a burning bush, and calls him by name. Then God tells him what He wants him to do. Wouldn't that be awesome? I mean, it was a hard job, but the part about God showing up, speaking to you, and giving clear instructions? God *has* called you to be His servant, but more often there's no burning bush or voice from heaven. Maybe a youth pastor has noticed a special gift in you. Perhaps the Lord has given you unique opportunities to serve. Or maybe you serve as you respond to what you read in scripture. Pay attention, because you and your gifts *matter* to God.

Lord, I long to be faithful in responding to You.
Show me how and where and who You've
called me to serve. Amen.

SAVED BY GRACE

It is by grace you have been saved, through
faith—and this is not from yourselves, it is the gift
of God—not by works, so that no one can boast.
Ephesians 2:8–9

Even though we know that Jesus saved us because He loves us, it can be really tempting to think that our faith depends on our good works. We slip into that trap when we believe that God is pleased with us because we spent hours in prayer, or volunteered at a nursing home, or shared the Gospel with a stranger. And while those no doubt delight God's heart, our salvation doesn't depend on them. And here comes the really good news: that assurance also means that when we fail, when we sin against God in small ways and big ones, we're *still* saved by God's grace. Isn't that great news? Regardless of your performance, God's got you.

God, thank You for the assurance that I am held in
Your loving grace, even when I fail. I am grateful that
my salvation depends on You and not me! Father,
I am humbled by Your grace. Amen.

GOD HEARS YOU, GOD SEES YOU

God heard their groaning and he remembered his covenant with Abraham, with Isaac and with Jacob. So God looked on the Israelites and was concerned about them.

EXODUS 2:24-25

Ever have one of those days when absolutely everything goes wrong? They might be small things, like slipping on the school bus, or spilling chocolate milk on your shirt, or getting your period during English class. (Okay, that's no small thing.) But you also might be facing bigger challenges. Maybe your grandmother is really really sick. Or maybe you crashed your mom's car. Or maybe your parents are considering getting divorced. Beloved, know that you are not alone. When God's people were suffering under slavery in Egypt, God saw. God heard. God cared. And God intervened. And today, God sees you, God hears you, God cares for you. You are held in God's love.

Lord, when I close my eyes and listen for Your voice,
I hear You saying, "I got you, girl." Thank You
that You are attentive and present to me.
I know I can trust You. Amen.

THE GIFT IN YOU

Do not neglect the gift which is in you. . .which was directly imparted to you [by the Holy Spirit]. . . . Practice and cultivate and meditate upon these duties; throw yourself wholly into them [as your ministry], so that your progress may be evident to everybody.
1 TIMOTHY 4:14–15 AMPC

Did you know that there's a gift inside you? There is. Maybe you already know what it is, and maybe you haven't yet discovered it. (Kind of exciting, right?) God has gifted you to be a builder of His kingdom, and whatever gift, or gifts, you've been given are meant to build up Christ's body. The gift you have might not be as glitzy as that of a nationally ranked gymnast or that girl who got a perfect score on her SAT. But your gift is needed for the body of Christ to be whole and healthy. Today, ask God what gift you've been given to bless others.

God, a lot of days I don't feel like I have much to give anyone. But I trust Your Word, and ask You to show me the gift or gifts You've given me, so that I might serve You and Your kingdom faithfully. Amen.

BE STILL, AND KNOW

He says, "Be still, and know that I am God; I will be exalted
among the nations, I will be exalted in the earth." The LORD
Almighty is with us; the God of Jacob is our fortress.

PSALM 46:10–11

If you're like a lot of teens, your daily schedule might be pretty crazy. You might hit the ground running before 7 a.m., and by the time clubs, school, sports, youth group, and homework are done, you're ready to crash. A lot of us are bombarded by obligations and responsibilities that keep our wheels spinning. But God is inviting you into something better. Whether you're on the school bus, or at McDonald's, or micro-waving your dinner, God whispers in your ear, "Be still, and know that I am God." God gives you the good reminder that He is God and you are not, and God also invites you to pause and be still. Set an alarm on your phone, or practice this pause with each meal: breathe deeply and say, "I am still. Because You are God."

Lord, You know how wound up I get! Thank You for the
gift of stillness that allows me to recognize You as the
One who is in charge of all things. Amen.

WASH ONE ANOTHER'S FEET

"If I then, the Lord and the Teacher, washed your feet,
you also ought to wash one another's feet. For I gave you
an example that you also should do as I did to you. . . .
If you know these things, you are blessed if you do them."
JOHN 13:14–15, 17 NASB

Back in the day, the job of foot-washing was reserved for lowly servants. So when Jesus stooped over to wash Peter's dusty, dirty feet, Peter resisted. But Jesus, who was modeling how His followers were to live, insisted on washing His friend's feet. And Jesus coached His friends to do for one another what He had done for them. What will "foot-washing" look like in your life? Maybe it will mean scrubbing a friend's feet before a mani-pedi, but it also might mean serving her in other ways: helping her with her homework, treating her to lunch, or showing up at her house after a family member dies. Ask God how you are being called to serve your friends in His name.

Jesus, thank You for showing us the best way to live.
Inspire and equip me, today, to live a life of love for
others the way that You did. Amen.

NOTICE WHAT GOD IS LIKE

But you, Lord, are a compassionate and gracious God, slow to anger, abounding in love and faithfulness. Turn to me and have mercy on me; show your strength in behalf of your servant.

PSALM 86:15-16

Throughout history it's been natural for human beings to assume that God is like a "person" on steroids. As a result, we expect God to be punishing like a judge, angry like our dad, judging like our mom, or critical like a grandparent. But the psalmist paints a picture of God that shows God to be *different* from a lot of the people in our lives. And the writer, who's experienced God's character, insists that God is compassionate and gracious. God doesn't explode in rage, but is slow to anger. God isn't stingy with love, but is abounding in love and faithfulness. Pause this week to meditate on God's gracious, loving, and faithful character.

Father, I thank You that You are different than every person I've encountered on my journey. Continue to reveal Your beautiful character to me, that I might know You, love You, and trust You. Amen.

WHEN GOD SAYS NO

Next Paul and Silas traveled through the area of Phrygia and Galatia, because the Holy Spirit had prevented them from preaching the word in the province of Asia at that time.
ACTS 16:6 NLT

I don't know about you, but when I want something, I want it *now*. Maybe it's a chocolate milkshake. Maybe it's an acceptance to a certain school. Or maybe it's a person I'd love to be dating. But sometimes God doesn't give me what I want when I want it. But when things didn't go the way that Paul and Silas expected them to go, scripture says that the Holy Spirit actually *prevented* it. And this makes me think that, in ways I can't always see, God prevents me from realizing or experiencing something that might not be God's best for me. And although I can't always know the reason, I do know that I can trust in God's goodness and in God's love for me.

Lord, You know the desires of my heart.
And although I don't understand why I can't have
what I want when I want it, I do trust that You know
and You are working for my good. Thank You
for protecting and loving me. Amen.

GOD IS MOVED BY PRAYER

After that God was moved by prayer.
2 SAMUEL 21:14 NASB

When was the last time you prayed, asking God for something *big*?! Maybe you were praying for someone who was ill. Or maybe you prayed for someone who was hungry or incarcerated. Or perhaps you prayed for one of the conflicts or wars unfolding around our globe. Scripture assures us that when we pray, God *hears* our prayers. And not only does God hear, but God is *moved* by your prayers. So what would be different in your life, today, if you lived daily as if God was persuaded and moved by your prayers? (I, for one, would pray *more*!) This week, choose one thing that's on your heart to offer to God daily, with the assurance that God hears and God cares.

God, I am amazed that You not only hear
my prayers but are moved by them. Today
I pray with boldness with the assurance
that You care and You respond.

19

IF YOU LOVE GOD, LOVE YOUR SISTERS AND BROTHERS

We love because he first loved us. Whoever claims to love God yet hates a brother or sister is a liar. For whoever does not love their brother and sister, whom they have seen, cannot love God, whom they have not seen. And he has given us this command: Anyone who loves God must also love their brother and sister.

1 JOHN 4:19–21

Have you ever met someone who was a pretty "religious" person, but was not kind to others? Maybe they *talked* a lot about God, but the behavior you saw them practicing toward other people gave you pause. Scripture is clear that if you love God, then loving the people around you is requisite. We can't love God, who we're not able to see, if we don't love people, who we *can* see. According to Jesus, loving others and loving God are inextricable. They can't be pulled apart.

*Spirit, quicken my heart to notice the faces of people
I have not loved well. Show me these precious ones,
and give me the courage to love them better.
Teach me to love the way Jesus loved. Amen.*

GOD CONSTANTLY REMEMBERS YOU

*"Can a woman forget her nursing child and have no compassion
on the son of her womb? Even these may forget, but I will not forget
you. Behold, I have inscribed you on the palms of My hands."*
ISAIAH 49:15–16 NASB

Have you ever babysat for an infant or spent time around a newborn
neighbor or relative? You'll notice that when that baby cries, its mother—
by birth or adoption—is eagerly attentive to his or her cry. In fact, moms
can even learn to distinguish the "hungry" cry from the "wet" cry from
the "sleepy" cry! So God uses this extreme example of attentive care to
say, "Even when the most reliable human love fails, that of a mom for a
newborn, my love *never* fails." God even promises that our names are
inscribed on the palms of His hands. Close your eyes and imagine your
name written across God's palm.

*God, thank You for teaching me what Your love is
like. And thank You for assuring me that even
when human loves fails, You never forget
me. I trust in Your love, amen.*

GOD SEES YOUR PAIN

A funeral procession was coming out as he approached the village gate. The young man who had died was a widow's only son, and a large crowd from the village was with her. When the Lord saw her, his heart overflowed with compassion.

LUKE 7:12–13 NLT

The Gospel writer Luke describes a funeral procession marching past as Jesus approached the city gate. It was a funeral of a young man who'd been his mother's only son. And on top of that, the woman was widowed. So it's fair to assume that this young man who died had been her whole world. And when Jesus saw her, "his heart overflowed with compassion." He noticed her tears. And when you are sad, beloved, God sees your tears as well. With that confidence, offer God the hurts in your heart today.

Lord, I thank You that You not only see the hurts of our hearts, but You care. I do believe that when You notice the hurts I carry, Your heart overflows with compassion. Thank You for Your tender love for me. Amen.

TRUST THAT GOD SEES YOUR PAIN

*"Do not fear or be dismayed because of this great multitude,
for the battle is not yours but God's."*
2 CHRONICLES 20:15 NASB

Sometimes we're asked to do something that seems *bigger* than we are. Maybe we're attempting to help others by raising a lot of money for a charity. Or maybe we have the rare opportunity to bless someone battling cancer by donating our blood marrow. Sometimes God puts big opportunities in front of us, and those opportunities require us to trust Him. When Jehoshaphat got word that a huge army was coming to attack the people of Judah, he sought the Lord. And the Lord assured Jehoshaphat that He would be with them in battle. God would help them do something bigger than they could do on their own.

*God, You know the challenges I am facing at home,
school, with friends, and with others. And although
I feel small, I am trusting in Your greatness.
I trust that You can help me do something
bigger than I can do on my own. Amen.*

I AM THE LORD'S SERVANT

"I am the Lord's servant," Mary answered.
"May your word to me be fulfilled." Then the angel left her.
LUKE 1:38

When you played with the little Fisher Price nativity set your parents pulled out each year in December, or made up stories with the wooden characters displayed on the fireplace mantel, you no doubt repeated the Christmas story you'd heard at home or at church. Mary gave birth to Jesus in a manger; cue the angels singing. But did you ever stop and say, "This is a really *crazy* story!" It's absurd because Mary was a teenager, just like you. And she was part of a community that expected a single young woman to *not* be pregnant. And although centuries later we're all on board with the story, it is certain that folks in her community would *not* have believed she was carrying God's child! In Mary we see a radical, beautiful faith in God lived out.

God, give me the heart of Mary. Help me to say
yes to Your will for my life, even when it means
courage, sacrifice, and even humiliation.
I put my trust in You. Amen.

GOD WAITING FOR YOU, YOU WAITING FOR GOD

So the LORD must wait for you to come to him so he can show
you his love and compassion. For the LORD is a faithful
God. Blessed are those who wait for his help.
ISAIAH 30:18 NLT

I don't know about you, but I'm not a big fan of waiting. If I feel like eating a cheeseburger, I zip through a drive-through window. If I want to watch a certain movie, I can order it online. If there's a dress I want, I can have it shipped to me in a few days. But God has invited us into a very different rhythm of life. The One who longs to show us His love and compassion *waits for us to come* to Him. Isn't that a beautiful picture? And we are called blessed when we make up our minds to slow down and wait for God's help. What will look different in your life when you decide to wait on God?

God, You know that if I were the boss, I wouldn't
choose to wait. But thankfully I'm not the boss!
And I trust completely in what You provide.
Grant me patience to wait on You. Amen.

COMMITTING TO PRAY FOR OTHERS

I urge, then, first of all, that petitions, prayers, intercession and thanksgiving be made for all people—for kings and all those in authority, that we may live peaceful and quiet lives in all godliness and holiness. This is good, and pleases God our Savior, who wants all people to be saved and to come to a knowledge of the truth.

1 TIMOTHY 2:1-4

In this day and age, a lot of people are quick to criticize. Whether it's a coach we don't like, the principal of our high school, or even those elected to federal office, a lot of us can be quick to condemn those who have authority over us. But the problem isn't a new one. And in Paul's letter to a young follower of Jesus named Timothy, he challenges the young man to pray—and pray in particular for those in authority. This, Paul insists, pleases God. Is there someone whom God is calling you to pray for?

Lord, You know that I long to live a life that's pleasing to You. Quicken my heart, by Your Spirit, to pray for those who lead, petitioning You, interceding, and giving thanks. Amen.

GOD HEARS YOU WHEN YOU CRY OUT

"If you take your neighbor's cloak as a pledge, return it by sunset, because that cloak is the only covering your neighbor has. What else can they sleep in? When they cry out to me, I will hear, for I am compassionate."
EXODUS 22:26–27

Sometimes when we pray it can be tempting to wonder if God is listening. At times it might feel like our prayers are just hitting the ceiling and not quite making it to God's ears! But throughout the scriptures we encounter a God who not only listens, but who is particularly attentive to those in need who cry out to Him. That's the person who has only one set of clothes. It's the person who's being oppressed. It's the one who must depend on God to be a deliverer. When you cry out to God with the needs of your heart, know that God hears your prayer and God cares.

God, I believe that You are listening. And I'm convinced that when I cry out to You, You hear and You care and You act. Today I put my faith in You and in Your kindness. Amen.

27

DO YOU WANT TO BECOME WELL?

When Jesus noticed him lying there [helpless], knowing that he had already been a long time in that condition, He said to him, Do you want to become well? [Are you really in earnest about getting well?]
JOHN 5:6 AMPC

The Gospel of John gives us a peek at an interaction Jesus had with a physically disabled man. The man was intent on finding help to get into a nearby pool when Jesus asked him, "Do you want to become well?" The man was seeking one thing, and Jesus asked him if he was up for something *even better*. That's us sometimes too, isn't it? We've set our mind on one thing, but Jesus has something even better in store for us. When Jesus healed this man, he picked up his mat and he *walked!* Today, lift your eyes off what has captured your attention and set them on Jesus. Look at His face and let Him know that you trust Him for what is best for your life.

Jesus, I admit that my vision is small. I set my sight on small goals, when You offer me abundance. Open my eyes so that I may see You and embrace what You have for me. Amen.

JESUS FEEDS THE HUNGRY

Jesus took the five loaves and two fish, looked up toward heaven,
and blessed them. . . . Afterward, the disciples picked up
twelve baskets of leftover bread and fish. A total of
5,000 men and their families were fed.
MARK 6:41, 43–44 NLT

One of the most famous miracles Jesus performs is the feeding of over five thousand people with just five little loaves of bread and two fish. Seriously, that could fit in one small backpack! But when his disciples asked him what to do about the huge hungry crowd, Jesus calmly instructed them to feed that big crew with what amounted to a little boy's lunch. Whether it's food, money, time, or something else, we naturally believe that what is possible depends on what we can see with our own eyes. But Jesus demonstrated that He can do much, much more than we can imagine. Where does Jesus want to increase your limited resources?

Jesus, just as You multiplied some bread and some
fish, I believe that You can make the most of
what I bring to You. So I offer You all I have,
expecting You to do a new thing. Amen.

DON'T WORRY ABOUT ANYTHING

Don't worry about anything; instead, pray about everything.
Tell God what you need, and thank him for all he has done.
Then you will experience God's peace, which exceeds
anything we can understand. His peace will guard
your hearts and minds as you live in Christ Jesus.
PHILIPPIANS 4:6-7 NLT

If you had to prioritize the biggest worries on your heart and mind, which ones would make the list? Passing the test to get your driver's license? Having a date for prom? Making it to—and through!—college? Or maybe there's something happening at home that is stressing you out. When the apostle Paul wrote a little letter to the Christian church in Philippi, he wanted to comfort them with the assurance that if anything was eating at them, they could pray about it. They could offer their worries to God and let Him know what they needed. And he even promised God's peace when we release our concerns to Him.

God, You probably know better than I do what
thoughts and worries are eating away at my heart
and mind. As Your Spirit prompts me,
I release them to You. Amen.

I KNOW I SHOULDN'T WORRY, BUT. . .

*"And why do you worry about clothes? See how the flowers of
the field grow. They do not labor or spin. Yet I tell you that not
even Solomon in all his splendor was dressed like one of these."*
MATTHEW 6:28–29

When Jesus was teaching crowds in His Sermon on the Mount, He asked
His audience, "Why do you worry about clothes?" Now, to be clear, the
first-century worries of folks who were most likely financially poor were
a little different than our fashion worries today. Often we're concerned
that we're wearing the latest or coolest fashion. Or we're checking to
see how something makes our bodies look. But a lot of folks in Jesus'
audience were struggling to keep a roof over their heads, food on the
table, and clothing on their kids' backs! And Jesus' comfort to them is
also His comfort to us today: *God will care for you.*

*God, I confess I worry about stuff I know doesn't
matter in the long run. But today, it feels like it does!
I offer my concerns and preoccupations
to You, in Jesus' name. Amen.*

WHEN FOES ATTACK

O God, have mercy on me, for people are hounding me.
My foes attack me all day long. . . . But when I am afraid,
I will put my trust in you. I praise God for what he has
promised. I trust in God, so why should I be afraid?
PSALM 56:1, 3-4 NLT

When we read what writers from hundreds of years ago wrote in the Psalms, it can be hard to relate to some of the struggles they faced: armies waging war, attacks by wild animals, or even the offering of religious sacrifices. But the confidence these writers expressed in God's undying faithfulness is something we can appropriate for ourselves. In Psalm 56, the writer who is hounded by attacks from his enemies places his trust in God. While your enemies might not have swords, it's possible they have a mouthful of sharp or threatening words for you. Whatever threat you face, you can trust in God as your helper.

God, You know the kinds of attacks to which I'm
vulnerable. And when I'm hounded, when I'm
afraid, I will put my trust in You. Amen.

WORDS THAT BRING LIFE

Every part of Scripture is God-breathed and useful one way or another—showing us truth, exposing our rebellion, correcting our mistakes, training us to live God's way. Through the Word we are put together and shaped up for the tasks God has for us.
2 TIMOTHY 3:16-17 MSG

Have you ever set out to read the Bible from cover to cover? Maybe it was your New Year's resolution or your summer project. A lot of folks who attempt this noble feat get mired in the muck halfway through Exodus, never even making it to Leviticus or Numbers—which come with their own challenges! And while the Bible does include all different kinds of writings—from history, to laws, to songs, to poems, to good old-fashioned letters—we're assured that every part of scripture is *useful* to us. So as you chew on scripture, doing your best to digest and appreciate God's holy Word, know that you are being nourished and strengthened for whatever it is that God has planned for you.

God, thank You for sending Your Spirit to breathe life into Your Word as I read it! Help me to hear Your voice and respond with obedience. Amen.

GOD'S LOVE IS STRONG

*As high as heaven is over the earth, so strong is his love
to those who fear him. . . . As parents feel for their children,
GOD feels for those who fear him. He knows us inside
and out, keeps in mind that we're made of mud.*
PSALM 103:11, 13 MSG

It would be kind of funny if you were made of mud, right? And yet—in this yummy Bible paraphrase from a writer named Eugene Peterson, called *The Message*—that's exactly what the psalmist is claiming. Other versions of scripture say that God remembers "we are dust." And while it's not the most flattering portrayal, the psalmist tenderly describes God as a parent who knows that we're fragile. Vulnerable. Weak. And knowing how we are, we discover that God's love for us is pretty big and strong.

*God, You know the places and ways I am weak.
And in my weakness, I am trusting that You are strong.
Be the parent who loves me and cares for me. Amen.*

BE CONFIDENT GOD HEARS YOU

I write these things to you who believe in the name of the Son of God so that you may know that you have eternal life. This is the confidence we have in approaching God: that if we ask anything according to his will, he hears us. And if we know that he hears us— whatever we ask—we know that we have what we asked of him.

1 JOHN 5:13–15

Sometimes when parents ask their kids to do a job around the house, the child might act as if she doesn't hear the parent. (So I've *heard*.) Or if a child asks a parent for money to go out with friends, that parent might act like they don't hear the child's request. But God's Word assures us that "if we ask anything according to his will, he hears us." Not only that, but we're told that when He hears us, and our prayers are within God's will, God delivers! What is it that you are asking of God this week?

*God, I confess I am shy to make requests of You.
And yet I'm emboldened by the promise that You hear
and I'm inspired by the assurance that You answer.
Hear the prayers of my heart and lips today. Amen.*

EVERY GOOD GIFT IS FROM GOD

Don't be deceived, my dear brothers and sisters. Every good and perfect gift is from above, coming down from the Father of the heavenly lights, who does not change like shifting shadows. He chose to give us birth through the word of truth, that we might be a kind of firstfruits of all he created.

JAMES 1:16–18

Have you ever worked really hard to earn money to buy something you really wanted? Maybe you babysat every weekend for four months to buy a laptop. Or you saved money from your job bussing tables to get a new phone. And it can be tempting to believe that we have good things because of our own efforts. But James says that when we believe that, we've deceived ourselves, since every good gift comes from God. So rather than applauding your own effort, remember to give thanks to the One who loves you and is a good and faithful Provider.

*God, You have blessed me abundantly with all
I need: food, shelter, clothing, education, family, love.
Thank You for being the giver of all good gifts. Amen.*

I'LL BE WITH YOU

*"I'm sending you to Pharaoh to bring my people, the People of Israel,
out of Egypt." Moses answered God, "But why me? What makes
you think that I could ever go to Pharaoh and lead the children
of Israel out of Egypt?" "I'll be with you," God said.*
EXODUS 3:10–12 MSG

The earliest chapters of the book of Exodus describe the unbearable conditions endured by God's people when they were slaves in Egypt. Graciously, God hears their cries and intervenes. And God's big plan is a guy named Moses. Although we often think of him as a superhero of sorts, he was really just a regular guy—not so different from you and me. So his question to God is one I think we'd ask too: "Why me?" And God's answer to Moses is also God's answer to us when He asks us to do big things: "I'll be with you." Hang on to those four holy words this week as you say yes to God.

*Lord, I confess that on most days I feel ill-equipped
to be Your person in the world. But I do believe
that You are with me. Give me courage today
to stand up for what's right. Amen.*

RESIST THE DEVIL, COME NEAR TO GOD

So be subject to God. Resist the devil [stand firm against him], and he will flee from you. Come close to God and He will come close to you.
JAMES 4:7-8 AMPC

Have your parents ever cautioned you to avoid spending too much time with certain friends, or maybe encouraged you to spend more time with other friends? What they know—maybe because they learned it the hard way!—is that we are shaped by those we spend time with. And what's good about that is that we can make smart choices that help us be the young women God made us to be. But it's not just our choices about hanging out with peers at school or church. We can choose, daily, to stand firm against the devil and his tricky ways, and we can also choose to draw near to God. James confirms that those choices *matter!*

Father, I know I'm not a beach ball tossed about on the ocean. Thank You for equipping and empowering me to resist the enemy and to stay close to You. Amen.

THE SECRET IN ALL CIRCUMSTANCES

I know what it is to be in need, and I know what it is to have plenty.
I have learned the secret of being content in any and every situation,
whether well fed or hungry, whether living in plenty or in want.
I can do all this through him who gives me strength.

PHILIPPIANS 4:12–13

When Paul wrote to the church in a city called Philippi, he told them a secret! And it is a powerful one. Paul had experienced great prestige and privilege as a Jewish religious leader before he came to know Christ. He knew what it was to live large. But after Jesus transformed his life, he suffered rejection and imprisonment for his faith. So he also knew what it felt like to be down and out. The secret to *both*, Paul claims, is the confidence that—in plenty and in want—Christ gives us strength.

Jesus, You know that I much prefer having plenty to
being in need! But I am confident that no matter what
I have, You give me strength each day to endure and
even to thrive. So I put my trust in You. Amen.

GOD OPENS OUR EYES TO HIS GOODNESS

God opened Hagar's eyes, and she saw a well full of water.
She quickly filled her water container and gave the boy a drink.
GENESIS 21:19 NLT

One of the harder stories in scripture is when Abraham kicks Hagar—the mother of Abraham's own son, Ishmael—and her boy out of the household, sending them into the desert with only some food and a skin of water. When the water was gone, Hagar wept and waited for Ishmael to die. But God heard the boy's cries and sent His angel to comfort and encourage Hagar. And when she opened her eyes, she saw a well full of water. And God continued to meet their needs, making Ishmael into the leader of a great nation. She discovered, and we're reminded, that a God who is good is faithful to show up for us in the most difficult circumstances.

God, You know the struggles and challenges I am
facing today. And just as You provided for Hagar
and Ishmael, I believe that You provide for me.
Thank You for Your faithfulness. Amen.

WHAT CAN PEOPLE DO TO ME?

So we say with confidence, "The Lord is my helper; I will not be afraid.
What can mere mortals do to me?" Remember your leaders, who spoke
the word of God to you. Consider the outcome of their way of life
and imitate their faith. Jesus Christ is the same
yesterday and today and forever.

HEBREWS 13:6–8

Have you ever been working on a brainteaser or logic puzzle, and struggled to come up with the answer? Maybe you set it aside for a while, and when you return to it, the answer comes as a serendipitous "aha" moment! You see from a fresh perspective, and the solution becomes evident. The author of Hebrews invites us into a moment like this. In our daily lives it's most natural to be concerned with the people around us: people we work for, people we live with, and even people who scare us. And in a cosmic inversion of perspective, the writer announces that "mortals" can't really undo him, because God is his helper. Today, God is your helper too.

God, You know the ways I worry about what might
happen to me. But because You are my helper, I will
not be afraid. I trust You with my life today. Amen.

41

AFTER THE FIRE AND THE WATER

*We went through fire and through water, but You brought us out
into a broad, moist place [to abundance and refreshment and the
open air]. . . . He brought me forth also into a large place. . .
because He was pleased with me and delighted in me.*
PSALM 66:12; 18:19 AMPC

It's been said that "into every life a little rain must fall." Which is kind
of a polite way of saying that things don't always go the way we'd like
them to! But sometimes it's not just rain; it's violent monsoons. And
sometimes we're not just a little warm; we've got our feet in the fire. And
the psalmist reminds us that God takes us through the most difficult
seasons of our lives and then brings us into a beautiful place of security
and freedom. And the psalmist believes that God is pleased with him
and even *delights* in him! When you look toward God's face, can you
see that gracious countenance shining on you?

*Thank You, God, that You've been present to every
moment of my life. I believe that if today is fiery
or rainy, You will deliver me into a good place,
because You can be trusted. Amen.*

THE GOOD GOD HAS FOR THOSE WHO LOVE HIM

We know that God causes everything to work together for the good of
those who love God and are called according to his purpose for them.
ROMANS 8:28 NLT

When we look around our homes, our communities, and even God's big
world, we see so many ways the world is broken. Families come apart.
Parents struggle to put food on the table. And entire nations face the
scourge of war. And the apostle Paul knew that the early Christians
were trying to make sense of the challenges they faced, which even
included violent persecution for their faith. And Paul promised them
that—for those who love God and are called by Him—everything works
together for good. But it's hard to see that some days, isn't it? It's hard to
see how the hardship we face can be transformed. But God sees what
we can't yet see.

Lord, a lot of what I see around me doesn't make
sense. I don't understand why people have to
suffer. But, like Paul, I am willing to trust You.
Today I trust that You are good. Amen.

WHAT TRULY SATISFIES

*"Come, all you who are thirsty, come to the waters; and you who
have no money, come, buy and eat! Come, buy wine and milk
without money and without cost. Why spend money on what
is not bread, and your labor on what does not satisfy?"*
ISAIAH 55:1-2

For a number of years, I knew that the food I was putting in my body probably wasn't the very best for me. Because I enjoy exercise, I was able to enjoy ice cream, pizza, and dollar-store snack cakes without gaining too much weight, but I knew that I wasn't nourishing my body in a way that would keep me healthy. So when my body went a little cuckoo, I had to change my diet, reluctantly returning to eating healthier less-processed foods. And I could almost hear God's loving invitation from this passage in Isaiah, inviting me into life that really is life. Though we're drawn to false substitutes, God is always inviting us to receive what truly satisfies.

*God, You know the ways I'm drawn to what doesn't
really satisfy my deep places. So I welcome Your
invitation into the good life You offer so freely.
Help me make good choices! Amen.*

GIVE IT TO GOD, BECAUSE HE CARES FOR YOU

Humble yourselves, therefore, under God's mighty hand,
that he may lift you up in due time. Cast all your
anxiety on him because he cares for you.

1 PETER 5:6–7

If we were to pause on any given day, we might notice that we're carrying a heavier load of burdens than we realize. Maybe we live with a low-key anxiety about what our futures might hold. And we might carry the stress of a relationship at home that isn't healthy. Or we might have an ongoing conflict with a friend. Or enemy! Or we might be worried about our own health or the health of someone we love. Graciously, the Lord doesn't expect us to carry this big load on our own. Instead, we're invited to "cast" our anxiety on God—which is a fancy way of saying "dump." God longs to receive all of our cares because He loves us.

Lord, thank You for Your love. And thank You
for receiving all the worries I have been carrying.
One by one, I give them to You. Today I
trust in Your love for me. Amen.

THIS HAPPENED FOR A REASON

"Neither this man nor his parents sinned," said Jesus, "but this happened so that the works of God might be displayed in him."
JOHN 9:3

When bad things happen to us, the first thing we naturally do is ask, "What did I do to deserve this?" If a boyfriend breaks up with us or we get in a car accident, our impulse can be to believe that we did something to "deserve" it. And that suspicion has been with us throughout history. In the first century, if someone was born with a disability, the community wondered if the parents or the child had sinned. But Jesus turns our suspicions upside down when He answers, "This happened so that the works of God might be displayed in him." If there's a situation in your life that you don't understand, ask God, "How will Your work be shown through this?"

God, I confess that I don't always understand Your ways. But I do trust that You love me and that You are good. Show me how Your goodness can be displayed through my life. Amen.

FOOD THAT NO ONE ELSE CAN SEE

I have food (nourishment) to eat of which you know nothing and have no idea. . . . My food (nourishment) is to do the will (pleasure) of Him Who sent Me and to accomplish and completely finish His work.

JOHN 4:32, 34 AMPC

When Jesus and His buddies were traveling through a Samaritan town called Sychar, they'd trudged off to the grocery store to find lunch, and Jesus had stayed behind. And in the most unlikely conversation between Jesus and a Samaritan woman—whom He shouldn't have spoken to because she was the wrong race, wrong religion, and wrong gender!—she comes to experience God's grace. And when His friends come back and are surprised by the interaction, they urge Jesus to eat. But He teaches His disciples that His food is to *please God!* And God was surely pleased, because many in the town believed in Jesus because of the woman's testimony. What is the work God has given you in which you find satisfaction?

Lord, give me an appetite to do Your will. Show me the kind of work You have prepared for me that will satisfy the deep hunger of my heart. Amen.

THE LORD CAUSES FLOURISHING

But the Lord was with Joseph, and he [though a slave] was a
successful and prosperous man. . . . And his master saw that
the Lord was with him and that the Lord made all
that he did to flourish and succeed in his hand.
GENESIS 39:2–3 AMPC

Sometimes we can be tempted to think that we'll finally be happy, or we'll finally be able to live out our purpose, once we reach some arbitrary milestone. Maybe we think we'll be happy if we get a boyfriend. Or we'll finally be happy once we're on our own at college. Or that we'll eventually get to live out God's purpose for our lives when we're in our twenties. But the witness of scripture is that God used a slave named Joseph to accomplish His purposes. Because Joseph was faithful right where was, God used him and blessed him. In what ways is God asking you to be faithful to Him right where you are?

God, some days I'd like my circumstances to be
different than they are. But I do trust that You can
use me, and want to use me, right where I am.
Be with me as I purpose to honor You! Amen.

THE ONE WHO NEVER LEAVES

*GOD went ahead of them in a Pillar of Cloud during the day to
guide them on the way, and at night in a Pillar of Fire to give
them light. . . . The Pillar of Cloud by day and the
Pillar of Fire by night never left the people.*
EXODUS 13:21–22 MSG

Most of us will experience ruptured relationships in our lives. Perhaps
we were relinquished for adoption as infants. Maybe we lost a parent
to divorce. Or a sibling to death. Or maybe we simply experience the
regular everyday bumps and bruises we experience in relationship with
others. And we long to be loved by One who never fails and never leaves
us. When God's people sojourned through the wilderness, His presence
among them was palpable: a pillar of cloud by day and a pillar of fire by
night. They could see with their eyes that God's presence was with them.
Although God no longer takes on physical form, we have the assurance
that, day or night, God never leaves us or forsakes us.

*God, You know that my heart longs for a steadfast love
that never fails. Thank You that I can depend on You.
I am grateful that You will never leave me. Amen.*

THE ONE WHO NOTICES OUR SORROWS

*You keep track of all my sorrows. You have collected all my
tears in your bottle. You have recorded each one in
your book. . . . This I know: God is on my side!*

PSALM 56:8–9 NLT

When we're hurting, it's tempting to believe that we are alone. That no
one cares. That we don't matter. But we have the assurance, in God's
Word, that He sees, He hears, He knows, and He cares. And the psalmist
announces that very promise in such beautiful words: "You keep track
of all my sorrows." What that means is that whatever hurts you experienced as a very young girl, maybe even before you can remember,
God keeps track of. And when others sin against you, God keeps track
of those offenses. And what's so very liberating about this promise is
that because God is keeping track, *we don't need to!* Instead, we have
the confidence that we can leave our hurts and wounds in God's care.

*This I know, God: You are on my side! And because
You are on my side, I don't have to nurse old hurts
or offenses. In this moment, I release
them into Your care. Amen.*

JESUS IS LOOKING FOR YOU

He wanted to see who Jesus was, but because he was short he could not see over the crowd. So he ran ahead and climbed a sycamore-fig tree to see him, since Jesus was coming that way. When Jesus reached the spot, he looked up and said to him, "Zacchaeus, come down immediately. I must stay at your house today." So he came down at once and welcomed him gladly.

LUKE 19:3-6

When we hear about God's love in church, some of us are quick to agree that God loves us. But in our deep places, we struggle to say, "I know that God loves *me*." It's easier for us to believe that God loves other people—especially the "good" people!—than that God loves us. But in a huge crowd, we see Jesus beeline toward the most unlikely guy you could imagine. Because Zacchaeus was a tax collector who exploited his neighbors for his own financial gain, everyone in his community hated him. And yet this is the person Jesus chose to spend time with!

Jesus, I thank You that You don't share the world's values! And thank You that You love me even more than I love myself some days. Help me receive Your love today. Amen.

51

GOD INVITES US AS BUILDERS OF HIS KINGDOM

Surely the Sovereign LORD does nothing without
revealing his plan to his servants the prophets.
AMOS 3:7

Before he was called by God to be a prophet, Amos was a farmer and a shepherd. Unlike many that God called as prophets, Amos wasn't from a school or lineage of prophets. And yet—as seems to be God's way!—God chose this unlikely candidate to speak on His behalf. And although God is sovereign, and does not depend on humankind to accomplish His will, Amos exclaims that God "does nothing without revealing His plan to His servants the prophets." God has chosen to use fragile human beings as partners in bringing forth His kingdom on earth as it is in heaven. And the method God established among His ancient people, He continued in the person of Jesus and today *in us!* How is it that God has called you to participate in building His kingdom?

Lord, it's crazy that You use people like Amos, and
people like me, to accomplish Your good purposes.
Help me to be faithful as a servant who
longs to please You. Amen.

REJOICE WHEN THE LOST ARE FOUND

*"Then he calls his friends and neighbors together and says,
'Rejoice with me; I have found my lost sheep.' I tell you that
in the same way there will be more rejoicing in heaven
over one sinner who repents than over ninety-nine
righteous persons who do not need to repent."*

LUKE 15:6–7

Have you ever felt as though church on Sunday mornings can feel like a club? It can be tempting to believe that the group we gather and worship with are like God's "insiders" and those outside the church's doors are "outsiders." And in a sense, it's true! But in a series of short stories, Jesus reveals God's heart for outsiders, saying that a shepherd will leave the ninety-nine insiders to go after that *one sheep* who's wandered away. As you think about the folks in your orbit at school, or in sports, or at your job, or in your neighborhood, who is that "one sheep" that God is so passionate about going after? How can you share God's love with that one?

*Good Shepherd, You have revealed Your heart for
the lost. Inspire me both to share Your passion
for those who are lost and also join You in
pursuing them in love! Amen.*

YOU HAVE BEEN CALLED BY NAME

Listen to the LORD who created you. . . . "Do not be afraid,
for I have ransomed you. I have called you by name; you are mine. . . .
From eternity to eternity I am God. No one can snatch anyone
out of my hand. No one can undo what I have done."

ISAIAH 43:1, 13 NLT

Did one of your parents ever have a pet name for you that you loved
to be called? Or maybe a friend gave you a special nickname that
makes you feel known and loved? When Isaiah invites us to listen to
the Lord's voice, God announces, "I have called you by name; you are
mine." It's as if God is saying, "I don't love you because your family goes
to church. I don't love you accidentally!" God knows you intimately
and has called you His own. (He might even have a special name for
you!) And God's calling, Isaiah assures us, is irrevocable. No one can
snatch us from God's loving care.

God, thank You for this assurance that I belong to You.
That I matter, personally, to You. I agree with the
truth that no one can snatch me from Your
hand. Today, let me walk with You. Amen.

LOVE YOUR ENEMIES

*"But love your enemies, do good to them, and lend to them
without expecting to get anything back. Then your reward
will be great, and you will be children of the Most High,
because he is kind to the ungrateful and wicked."*

LUKE 6:35

Have you ever seen a movie where a feud between rival street gangs is perpetuated because members seek to avenge the wrongs done to them by their enemies? There are also nations around the world where generations have warred against one another, continuing to seek revenge for centuries. As human beings, it's how we're naturally wired. But Jesus, the radical Teacher, introduces a new way of living. Jesus-style love does good to those who threaten us. And it lends to those who oppose us without any expectation of return. Is there a relationship in your life where Jesus in inviting you to practice a surprising kind of love?

*Jesus, You know the folks in my life who are the
hardest for me to love. Send Your Spirit to equip
and inspire me to love them the way that
You love them, for Your sake. Amen.*

YOU ARE LOVED WITH AN EVERLASTING LOVE

The LORD appeared to us in the past, saying: "I have loved you with an everlasting love; I have drawn you with unfailing kindness."
JEREMIAH 31:3

The English language has lots of different uses for the word *love*. We *love* chocolate. We *love* our grandparents. We *love* God. We *love* our family pet. One word means a wide variety of different things! But the Hebrew word for God's love that's used in the Old Testament is a particular kind of love. And that word is *hesed*. God's *hesed* kind of love isn't the kind of love we might feel for a minute if we have a crush on a boy! Rather, the word indicates a steadfast, faithful, enduring love. A love with substance. A love that lasts. And that is the *kind* of love with which God loves you and loves me.

Lord, I thank You that Your love for me is of a different order than any of the other loves I've known. I thank You that I matter to You and that I can depend on Your unfailing love. Amen.

GOD NEVER FORGETS YOU

"What is the price of five sparrows—two copper coins? Yet God does not forget a single one of them. And the very hairs on your head are all numbered. So don't be afraid; you are more valuable to God than a whole flock of sparrows."

LUKE 12:6-7 NLT

In the ancient world, sparrows weren't expensive to purchase. In fact, today we might say that they were "a dime a dozen." And the small price tag suggests the possibility that these birds were insignificant or without much value. But Jesus insists to His listeners that God remembers every one of them. (That's kind of like saying He knows and remembers every mosquito in a big swarm of mosquitoes!) God doesn't forget a single one, and God does not forget you. Jesus goes on to say that not only does God remember us, but He even knows how many hairs are on our heads. Jesus tells these stories because He is convinced that we are precious to God, and He wants us to receive that in our deep places.

Lord, some days it's hard to believe that I am precious and valuable to You. Thank You for Your Word, through the lips of Your Son, insisting that I am worthy in Your sight. Amen.

BEING WISE TOWARD OTHERS

Be wise in the way you act toward outsiders; make the most of every opportunity. Let your conversation be always full of grace, seasoned with salt, so that you may know how to answer everyone.

Colossians 4:5–6

Have you ever thought about what those who aren't Christians think when they look at those who are followers of Jesus? While I'm sure there's a whole range of thoughts, I do know, as the apostle Paul did, that they do notice how we behave. They listen to the way we speak about others. They notice how we spend our money. They watch to see how we treat those on the world's margins. Naturally, they *notice*. When Paul was coaching the early Christians in Colossai in how to live faithfully, he coached them in how to behave toward those who aren't a part of the body of Christ. And he encouraged them to "be wise." This week, make the most of opportunities you have to display Christ living in you.

God, give me wisdom. I long to represent You well to those who are outside the faith. Give me grace so that I might speak well and love well. Amen.

THOUGH YOU FALL, THE LORD SUPPORTS YOU

The steps of a [good] man are directed and established by the
Lord when He delights in his way [and He busies Himself with his
every step]. Though he falls, he shall not be utterly cast down,
for the Lord grasps his hand in support and upholds him.
PSALM 37:23-24 AMPC

Sometimes we can mistakenly believe that after we give our lives to God, we'll never stumble and fall again. We won't sin. We won't make mistakes. We won't suffer. But unfortunately, that's not how the life of faith works. The psalmist describes the person who trusts God, who is led by the Lord. This one is intent on following God, but—like you and I—is also someone who will face challenges and missteps. But the psalmist announces, "The Lord grasps his hand in support and upholds him." This week, when you most need God's help, notice the ways God grasps *your* hand and supports you.

Lord, You know that I long to walk faithfully with You.
When I stumble, when I sin, when I suffer, hold my
hand. I look to You to be my strong support. Amen.

LET GOD TRANSFORM YOU INTO A NEW PERSON

Don't copy the behavior and customs of this world, but let God transform you into a new person by changing the way you think. Then you will learn to know God's will for you, which is good and pleasing and perfect.

ROMANS 12:2 NLT

The timeless truth Paul shares with the early believers in Rome makes me wonder if he might have had a crystal ball to peek forward more than twenty centuries and see what our lives are like! Although he had no way of imagining the ways that social media, streaming movies, or music apps would shape the way we think, his wisdom for believers is spot on. His appeal to his peers could be his appeal to teen girls today: "You weren't made to be shaped by the world around you; God is transforming you into someone new by changing the way you think!" As you pray, ask God how He wants to transform your mind.

God, I thank You that I am Yours. And I offer all that I am to You. Send Your Spirit to guide me as I seek to honor You. Amen.

FINDING REST IN GOD

Truly my soul finds rest in God; my salvation comes from him.
Truly he is my rock and my salvation; he is my
fortress, I will never be shaken.

PSALM 62:1-2

Have you ever noticed that there are some people who may not have a lot happening in their lives, but they can often seem harried and unglued? And there are also some folks who have pretty rich and full lives who don't seem too stressed? That's because some of those people whose schedules are full know how to find the *rest* they need. Ideally that includes eight hours of sleep a night. But for those who've learned to trust God, it means that they turn to Him to find rest for their souls. When life feels overwhelming, they tip their faces toward God who is their rock. "I will never be shaken" is the ancient way of saying, "God's got me. I won't come undone." When you feel overwhelmed, pause and look to your rock.

Lord, You are truly a strong fortress. Thank You
that You are a reliable helper when I'm in
over my head. I put my trust in You. Amen.

SINCE GOD LOVES US. . .

This is love: not that we loved God, but that he loved us and sent his Son as an atoning sacrifice for our sins. Dear friends, since God so loved us, we also ought to love one another. No one has ever seen God; but if we love one another, God lives in us and his love is made complete in us.
1 JOHN 4:10–12

It would be really natural to reason that because God is invisible, we don't know what God is like. Super reasonable! Except. . .we do know what God is like. In God's love for us, we've learned God's character. And because we know what God's character is like, and the way God loves, we're charged to *love others like that.* The kind of love God has shown for us is sacrificial, and God expects us to love others sacrificially. Maybe we'll share our money with others. Or maybe we'll give from our time and talents. But the Word reminds us that true love will cost us something. Just as it cost God.

Lord, I long to love others the way that You have loved me. Quicken my heart so that I might love sacrificially, in Your name and for Your sake. Amen.

THE SHEEP KNOW HIS VOICE

"I am the good shepherd; I know my sheep and my sheep know me—just as the Father knows me and I know the Father—and I lay down my life for the sheep. I have other sheep that are not of this sheep pen. I must bring them also. They too will listen to my voice, and there shall be one flock and one shepherd."

JOHN 10:14-16

Have you ever heard someone say that they received a direct word from God, either audibly or in their spirit? I have, and I've always felt jealous! When He introduced Himself as the Good Shepherd, Jesus announced that His sheep know the sound of His voice. It must be nice, right? But guess what? You and I actually can hear God's voice speaking to us. We know exactly what it sounds like, because it has been made plain through the words of scripture. As you seek God, listen for His gentle word to you that is spoken clearly through His Word.

Lord, You know how I long to hear Your voice.
Thank You for Jesus, who has spoken plainly,
and for the clarity of Your written word.
Speak, Lord, for Your servant is listening. Amen.

GOT A PROBLEM? PRAY

Is anyone among you in trouble? Let them pray. Is anyone happy?
Let them sing songs of praise. Is anyone among you sick?
Let them call the elders of the church to pray over them
and anoint them with oil in the name of the Lord.

JAMES 5:13-14

In the early church, Christians were figuring out what it looked like to live as Jesus-followers after He'd ascended to be with the Father. And a lot of those little letters in the New Testament are some of the leaders of the church *coaching* the believers in how to live faithfully. And James wants Christians to know that—in whatever they are facing—they should pray. And in a series of three exhortations, he's kind of sandwiched "pray when happy" between "pray when in trouble" and "pray when sick." And that wasn't accidental! We're really motivated to pray when things aren't going our way, and James is reminding us to turn toward God even when life is good.

God, thank You for the privilege of bringing our whole
lives before You. Quicken my heart to come to You
when life is hard and when it's good. Amen.

WHAT GIVES GOD PLEASURE

His pleasure is not in the strength of the horse, nor his delight
in the legs of the warrior; the LORD delights in those who
fear him, who put their hope in his unfailing love.
PSALM 147:10–11

In the 1981 movie *Chariots of Fire*, 1924 Olympic gold medalist Eric Liddell famously said, "God made me fast. And when I run, I feel His pleasure." Isn't that beautiful? And it begs the question: *What gives God pleasure?* The psalmist asserts that God doesn't delight in the same things that give humans pleasure. "The strength of the horse" and "the legs of the warrior" might be the old-fashioned way of saying "fast cars" and "beautiful people." What gives God delight is those who fear Him and trust in His unfailing love. Regardless of his skill, that was the heart of Eric Liddell! And it is the heart of those who fear and trust God today.

Lord, although I confess that I'm tempted to value all
the things my culture values, I know that Your priorities
are different. Give me a heart that fears You and trusts
in Your unfailing love. You are my hope! Amen.

GOD HAS DESIGNED WORK WITH YOUR NAME ON IT

For we are God's handiwork, created in Christ Jesus to do good works, which God prepared in advance for us to do.
EPHESIANS 2:10

When God was creating you, imagining the unique, rare, one-of-a-kind human you would be, He created you with passions and gifts He would use in the building of His kingdom. Pretty cool, huh? For some of us, those might be creative gifts like writing or visual art or music. Others are knit together with a passion for loving and serving those who are too often relegated to the world's margins. And others might have entrepreneurial gifts or business savvy to create businesses that build the kingdom. Today you might have a hunch at how you've been wired, or you may still be discovering how God has made you. In either case, know that God has work for you to do that only you can do!

*God, my heart longs to serve You. And I know
that not every assignment has my name on it.
So continue to lead me and show me the
work You've cut out for me to do. Amen.*

GOD WILL GUARD YOU IN ALL YOUR WAYS

If you say, "The LORD is my refuge" and you make the Most High your dwelling, no harm will overtake you, no disaster will come near your tent. For he will command his angels concerning you to guard you in all your ways.

PSALM 91:9-11

As you think back on your life, when was a time you were most afraid? (If thinking about it feels scary, know that God is with you *right now*.) Maybe it was a time when you felt physically unsafe. Or maybe it was a season when you were scared about what the future might hold. Or perhaps you were afraid of losing someone you loved. At that time, you may or may not have known that God was with you. The psalmist says that God protects those who trust in Him. That means that no matter what you face, God is with you. God sees. God hears. God knows. God cares.

Lord, I need You to be my good protector. And I believe that You have never left me alone. Be present with me this day, and especially in the moments when I feel most scared. Amen.

67

BY THIS THEY'LL KNOW YOU'RE MINE

"A new command I give you: Love one another. As I have loved you,
so you must love one another. By this everyone will know that
you are my disciples, if you love one another."

JOHN 13:34-35

In the first century, Jesus was known by the communities He visited as a wise rabbi or teacher. Some of what He shared was the ancient wisdom given to God's people in the Old Testament. And some of what He taught turned the old teachings on their head! Whenever the Law, ritual, or revenge kept people bound, Jesus taught a new way of grace and freedom. And at the end of His earthly ministry, He gave them one more new command. It was kind of like His parting words—the thing that they couldn't *not* know! "A new command I give you," He offered, "Love one another." When you think of the way that Jesus loved others, how will you love those around you this week?

Jesus, You have loved me perfectly! And that is
the love to which I aspire. Teach me to love
those around me like You love me. Amen.

THE GOOD NEWS ABOUT TEMPTATION

So, if you think you are standing firm, be careful that you don't fall!
No temptation has overtaken you except what is common to mankind.
And God is faithful; he will not let you be tempted beyond what
you can bear. But when you are tempted, he will also
provide a way out so that you can endure it.
1 Corinthians 10:12–13

A lot of us joke freely that we're tempted by chocolate. (I know I am! Fudge brownie sundae, please.) But we also face other temptations, don't we? Maybe it's easy for us to lose our tempers and go off on others. Perhaps we're suddenly tempted when we see an opportunity to cheat on a test. Or maybe we've struggled to stay pure sexually. Scripture reassures us that we don't face any temptation that others aren't also facing. And we also have the assurance that when we are tempted, God always provides a way out. That's reassuring, right? So when you're in that bind, ask God to show you the way out.

Lord, You know the ways I struggle. But I long to live
faithfully for You. Send Your Spirit as a guide to
show me how to conquer temptation. Amen.

WHAT WAS MEANT FOR HARM, GOD INTENDED FOR GOOD

"So it was God who sent me here, not you! . . . You intended to harm me, but God intended it all for good. He brought me to this position so I could save the lives of many people."
GENESIS 45:8; 50:20 NLT

Do you know the story of Joseph in the Old Testament? (Not Jesus' dad, but someone who lived centuries earlier!) It is a *rough* story. After Joseph's brothers sold him into slavery, he was accused of sexual assault by the wife of his master! Thrown into prison, life was not looking good for Joseph. And in a crazy turn of events, while using the gifts God had given him while he was in prison, Joseph was not only released, but he became a powerful ruler in Egypt! And the lesson Joseph gleaned from his suffering is one we can learn from today: *what people intended for harm, God intended for good.* How does God want to redeem your difficult circumstances to bless others?

God, I don't pretend to understand some of the hard things I've faced. But I do trust that You love me and You can use what I've endured for good. Amen.

NO SERVANT IS GREATER THAN HIS MASTER

"Very truly I tell you, no servant is greater than his master, nor is a messenger greater than the one who sent him. Now that you know these things, you will be blessed if you do them."

JOHN 13:16–17

Some of us were raised on good old-fashioned Disney fairy tales: *Beauty and the Beast, Cinderella, The Princess and the Frog,* and others. And whether it was the cartoon feature films we watched as children or the rom coms we watch today, the story we've been told is that we deserve to be happy. And while it is true that God wants good for us, that good God desires may look a little different than what our culture is peddling. The thing we're made for, Jesus teaches, is to live the way He lived. If He is our Master, then our lives should be patterned after the servant-leader He was. As you think about the life you want to live, and the future you want to build, ask God how you can live more like Jesus.

God, only You know what my future holds. But I do ask You to transform me more and more into the image of Jesus. Teach me to love like He loved. Amen.

I AM FOR YOU

*In my distress I prayed to the LORD, and the LORD answered me
and set me free. The LORD is for me, so I will have no fear.*
PSALM 118:5-6 NLT

As a young adult, I was revisiting some of the hurts I experienced earlier in life. I raised my fist to God and demanded an explanation. Where were You? Where were those who should have protected me? And in a once-in-a-lifetime moment, I heard God whisper four words to my heart, "I am for you." Those words sunk deep, and I continue to chew on them today. Although they're not strung together in that order anywhere in scripture, I read them on every page! And the psalmist who wrote Psalm 118 confirms, "The LORD is for me, so I will have no fear." Beloved, do you know in your deep places that God is *for* you? If you're not yet convinced, invite God to confirm that truth to your heart.

*Lord, I long to experience, in my bones, the reality that
You are with me and You are for me. Minister to
my heart so that I might experience Your
great, great love. Amen.*

A FATHER'S LOVE

"The son said to him, 'Father, I have sinned against heaven and against you. I am no longer worthy to be called your son.' But the father said to his servants, 'Quick! Bring the best robe and put it on him. Put a ring on his finger and sandals on his feet. Bring the fattened calf and kill it. Let's have a feast and celebrate.'"
LUKE 15:21-23

When we approach God as a *Father*, it's not uncommon to expect God to react the way a human parent would in the same situation. It makes sense, right? And that's why Jesus goes to such great lengths, and tells such fabulous stories: Jesus wants us to know the love of a perfect father. Because when we mess up, especially after disrespecting our parents, they don't always respond with compassionate understanding. Not only does the father Jesus described offer his wayward child compassion, he throws a party to celebrate his return! Jesus wants us to know that our heavenly Father rejoices—no matter what we have done—when we return to Him.

Father, I thank You that Your love is unlike any other. And that no matter how or how often I've failed, You embrace me in Your loving arms when I return to You. Amen.

THE LORD LOOKS AT THE HEART

When they arrived, Samuel saw Eliab and thought, "Surely the LORD's anointed stands here before the LORD." But the LORD said to Samuel, "Do not consider his appearance or his height, for I have rejected him. The LORD does not look at the things people look at. People look at the outward appearance, but the LORD looks at the heart."

1 SAMUEL 16:6–7

Did you look in the mirror this morning? Did you put on makeup? Have you taken a selfie? Chances are good you've done one of those things! Our culture places a lot of value on people's appearances, especially girls' and women's. And throughout the Bible, we hear a message that turns our culture's values upside down. When Samuel looked on the tall, strong young men who were Jesse's sons, he assumed one of them would be God's choice. But the Lord reminded Samuel that His values aren't the same as the world's values. Among Jesse's sons, God had chosen David—the youngest and the smallest!—to rule over Israel.

God, I confess that I'm tempted to share the world's values about appearances. But Your Word reminds me that You look on the heart. Teach me to love and serve You with a pure heart.

JESUS SEES YOUR FAITH

Some men came, bringing to him a paralyzed man, carried by four of them. Since they could not get him to Jesus because of the crowd, they made an opening in the roof above Jesus by digging through it and then lowered the mat the man was lying on. When Jesus saw their faith, he said to the paralyzed man, "Son, your sins are forgiven."

MARK 2:3-5

In one of the craziest scenes in scripture, a group of friends decide to bring their friend—a man who was paralyzed and unable to walk—to Jesus. Because the crowd was so dense, they had to climb onto someone's roof, pull apart an opening in the roof, and lower their friend in front of Jesus, using the mat he'd been lying on. Pretty absurd, right? But when Jesus saw that guy being hoisted through the *ceiling*, He could see the faith those guys had in Him. And in response, Jesus both forgave the man's sins and also healed his body.

Jesus, You are a faithful healer! Give me the faith of these four friends as I seek healing in my life and as I bring my own friends before You. Amen.

YOUR WORDS ARE EVER BEFORE ME

*You, through Your commandments, make me wiser than
my enemies, for [Your words] are ever before me.*
PSALM 119:98 AMPC

Every day we show up at school, have dinner with our families, hang out with our friends, worship at church, go to our jobs, and compete in sports and other activities we have to figure out how to *live well*. And the author of Psalm 119 has figured out how to do that. In every verse of this long Psalm, which is 176 verses long, the writer says a version of the very same thing. The gist of every single verse is this, "God, because Your words and Your ways are true, they give me life." (Seriously, go check it out! It's intense.) The writer who has found life in God's words and God's ways is inviting you to do the same.

*Lord, I really believe that the wisdom I find in Your
Word can help me thrive and flourish. Grant me
a passion for scripture so that I might learn
from the wisdom You offer. Amen.*

IF YOU KNOW ME, YOU KNOW HIM

Thomas said to him, "Lord, we don't know where you are going, so how can we know the way?" Jesus answered, "I am the way and the truth and the life. No one comes to the Father except through me. If you really know me, you will know my Father as well. From now on, you do know him and have seen him."

JOHN 14:5-7

After Jesus announced that He was going to prepare a room for His disciples in His Father's house, Thomas just wanted to know how to get there. A legit concern in my book. And instead of dropping a pin to the location, Jesus told him, "If you really know me, you will know my Father as well." Heavy stuff! And those words are a gift for us today as well: if we want to know what the Father is like, and how He behaves, we have only to look at Jesus. What do you learn about the Father by knowing Jesus?

Father, thank You that You've revealed yourself through the person of Jesus. And thank You that my longing to know You and Your character is satisfied as I encounter Him. Amen.

77

THEN YOU WILL KNOW THAT I AM THE LORD

"I will attach tendons to you and make flesh come upon you and cover you with skin; I will put breath in you, and you will come to life. . . . Then you, my people, will know that I am the LORD, when I open your graves and bring you up from them."
 EZEKIEL 37:6, 13

When the Lord showed Ezekiel a valley of dry bones, He showed His prophet the condition of Israel's heart. As a people, they'd defiled themselves with idols and other sinful offenses, which had caused spiritual death. That's what happens when we sin, right? We choose death over life. But despite their sin, God is eager to redeem the people He loves. And He promises that when He brings them back to life, they'll recognize Him again as Lord. Today it's God's Holy Spirit who shows us our sin, who reveals the death and decay in our lives and guides us into redemption. Is there a way God is showing you places in your life that He wants to live again?

God, although it can be painful, I thank You for the gift of Your Spirit. Show me where I've sinned, and transform my heart, for Your glory. Amen.

I WILL WALK AMONG THEM

*"They will no longer defile themselves with their idols and vile images
or with any of their offenses, for I will save them from all their sinful
backsliding, and I will cleanse them. They will be my people, and I
will be their God. . . . My dwelling place will be with them;
I will be their God, and they will be my people."*

EZEKIEL 37:23, 27

God's prophets often had the hard job of pointing out the sin of God's
people and calling them to repentance. No one asks for this stinky job,
right? But it has to be done. And through the prophets, God often also
announced the promise of His presence with His people, both in their
sin and in their redemption. And through Ezekiel, God announced,
"My dwelling place will be with them; I will be their God and they will
be my people." The promise was true in Ezekiel's day. It most certainly
proved true when Jesus came to walk among us. And today God is
present with us through His Spirit. Beloved, no matter what you face,
you belong to God.

*Lord, thank You for the promise of Your presence.
You are my God and I am Your daughter! I rejoice
that You are abiding with me today. Amen.*

WE HAVE ACCESS TO THE FATHER

For it is through Him that we both [whether far off or near] now have an introduction (access) by one [Holy] Spirit to the Father [so that we are able to approach Him].
 EPHESIANS 2:18 AMPC

If you've ever been to a concert venue, you know that there is limited access to the performers. If you've paid your money for a ticket, you can access the seat you paid for, but you can't go backstage, before or after the show, to meet the band. But perhaps you've seen people wearing an "All Access" badge, allowing them to skirt around the rope, pass the gate, or go through the door. In his letter to the early Church in Ephesus, Paul assures the believers that because of Jesus, we have access to God through the Holy Spirit. That means that we can approach God boldly, knowing that we are authorized and will be received.

God, I am in awe that, because of Jesus, I can approach You with boldness. Thank You for inviting me to know You and be known by You. Amen.

DON'T LET ANYONE LOOK DOWN ON YOU BECAUSE YOU'RE YOUNG

*Don't let anyone look down on you because you are young, but set an
example for the believers in speech, in conduct, in love, in faith
and in purity. Until I come, devote yourself to the public reading
of Scripture, to preaching and to teaching. Do not neglect your
gift, which was given you through prophecy when the
body of elders laid their hands on you.*

1 TIMOTHY 4:12–14

As a young person, you probably notice when an adult believes in you.
When she celebrates your gifts. Or when he cheers you on toward your
next accomplishment. Well that's exactly what's happening in this letter
that Paul writes to Timothy, who was believed to be about sixteen years
old at the time. Paul is reminding Timothy that because he's been gifted
by God to minister in the name of Jesus, he shouldn't worry about anyone
who looks down on him because he's young. Instead, says Paul, set an
example for them in the way you live!

*Father, I know that not everyone takes me seriously
because I'm young. But because You've given me
gifts to serve You, I commit myself to using
those gifts for Your sake. Amen.*

THINK ABOUT THAT

Blessed be the Lord, Who bears our burdens and carries us day by day, even the God Who is our salvation! Selah [pause, and calmly think of that]!
PSALM 68:19 AMPC

Although they're printed in standard black font in the middle of our Bibles, the Psalms are actually a collection of songs and poems that were meant to be sung! It's really more like a hymnbook or PowerPoint slide meant to guide worshippers than anything else. And one of the ancient words that's used in the Psalms, the word *selah*, has been a little tricky for scholars and theologians to pin down. But this translation of scripture offers a pretty good guess, suggesting it means "pause, and calmly think of that." It's almost like punctuation, underscoring or adding emphasis, reminding the worshipper to really take note. If we choose to use the exclamation in our daily lives—in our morning devotions, while using a Bible app on our phones, or at our family's mealtime prayer—it can remind us to *pause* and notice what God has done.

God, embed the idea of "Selah"—or pausing to notice You—into my heart. By Your Spirit, open my eyes and ears to Your goodness and power and mercy. Amen.

SET YOUR HEARTS ON THINGS ABOVE

Since, then, you have been raised with Christ, set your hearts on
things above, where Christ is, seated at the right hand of God.
Set your minds on things above, not on earthly things.

COLOSSIANS 3:1–2

Some of what we read in the Bible is very particular to the cultural context of the ancient word. We don't always understand the weights and measures, geography, or politics that are mentioned in scripture. But more of what we discover in God's Word is timeless wisdom that spans human history. And human beings being consumed by what we can see and hear and touch is one of those things! We're tempted to set our hearts on this pair of jeans, or that laptop, or those shoes, or that phone. But, just like believers in the first century, we're invited to set our hearts—which really means our minds and our attention—on things that are not "earthly." When we set our minds on Christ, we're being who God made us to be.

Lord, You know how easily distracted I am by the
things of this world. Instead, today, quicken my heart
to seek Your face and listen for Your voice. Amen.

WHEN YOU GIVE, YOU'RE BLESSED

Give, and [gifts] will be given to you; good measure, pressed down, shaken together, and running over, will they pour into [the pouch formed by] the bosom [of your robe and used as a bag]. For with the measure you deal out [with the measure you use when you confer benefits on others], it will be measured back to you.

LUKE 6:38 AMPC

Have you ever met someone who was a generous giver? Maybe you have a friend who's happy to cover your meal when you're out together and you're broke. Or maybe you've seen your parents give generously to organizations who are doing great work. As Christians, we were made to share with others from the resources God has given us. And in the Gospels Jesus specifically says that the degree to which we *give* is the degree to which we'll *receive*. Pretty powerful, huh? If you've ever been afraid that by giving you won't have enough for yourself, practice giving this week in a way that stretches you a little bit, and notice what God does.

*God, scripture suggests that Your economy is different
than the one under which many of us often operate.
As I give generously to others, I trust
You to meet my needs. Amen.*

SPEAKING UP AT SUCH A TIME AS THIS

If you keep silent at this time, relief and deliverance shall arise for the Jews from elsewhere, but you and your father's house will perish. And who knows but that you have come to the kingdom for such a time as this and for this very occasion?
ESTHER 4:14 AMPC

In the Old Testament, we read a story that is as unlikely as a house-maid like Cinderella becoming a princess. When the king of Persia was seeking a new wife, a Jewish woman named Esther was selected for her beauty. But when the Jewish people in Persia were being oppressed, Esther had a decision to make. And her uncle, Mordecai, encouraged her to be brave and speak up for her people who were in grave peril. In fact, he suggested to her that God may have positioned her for that very moment. Is there some way today that God is calling you to be brave by speaking up?

Lord, I thank You for the witness of Esther. She shows me what it looks like to fear You instead of fearing men and women. Give me the courage to speak the words You put in my heart. Amen.

HE TOLD ME EVERYTHING I DID

Many of the Samaritans from that town believed in him because of the woman's testimony, "He told me everything I ever did." So when the Samaritans came to him, they urged him to stay with them, and he stayed two days. And because of his words many more became believers.

JOHN 4:39-41

In an unlikely exchange with a pretty unlikely woman, Jesus confronts a Samaritan woman with the truth about her life. When she claims to have no husband, Jesus agrees and announces that she's actually had five husbands, and the guy that she was with at the time was not her husband. This is a woman he'd never met before! While a lot of people would feel pretty defensive about a stranger calling them out like that, she actually experienced the exchange with Jesus as a loving one, and told others about what had happened. As a result, many believed.

Jesus, I thank You that You know me inside and out—even the parts of my life I'm not proud of. I thank You for Your grace and for receiving me exactly as I am. Amen.

WAIT FOR THE LORD

Those who wait for the Lord [who expect, look for, and hope in Him]
shall change and renew their strength and power; they shall lift
their wings and mount up [close to God] as eagles [mount up
to the sun]; they shall run and not be weary, they shall
walk and not faint or become tired.

ISAIAH 40:31 AMPC

Maybe you've heard this passage of scripture from Isaiah before. The word *wait*, in this instance, means more than waiting in line for a burger or to get your driver's license. This kind of waiting is to put your hope and your trust in what God provides. It's kind of like saying, "Instead of trusting in my good grades, or my admirable behavior, or my performance on the field, I'm going to put all my confidence in God." It was radical then, and it's radical now. And God promises that those who do wait on Him will not wear out, but will be renewed and restored.

God, most of the people I know trust in what they can
manage themselves: their incomes, their reputation,
their networks, their achievements. But I put all
of my hope and trust in You. Amen.

ONE THING LASTS FOREVER

For, "All people are like grass, and all their glory is like the flowers of the field; the grass withers and the flowers fall, but the word of the Lord endures forever." And this is the word that was preached to you.
1 PETER 1:24–25

After America's Great Depression, the De Beers diamond company had to find a way to sell their wares. In 1948 copywriter Mary Frances Gerety presented her pitch for the campaign to the advertising company she worked for, suggesting the slogan, "A Diamond is Forever." The slogan was a hit then, and remains in use today! I suspect it appeals to the human longing for eternity in our hearts. But God's Word says that only one thing lasts forever, and it ain't diamonds. Most things fade, Peter writes, but God's Word endures forever. Reminding the Church to let go of what doesn't last, he exorts them to hang on to what matters most.

Lord, I thank You for Your Word, and I thank You that it is not fleeting like the flowers that fall to the ground. Today I trust in the promise and hope I find in Your Word. Amen.

YOU ARE GOD'S CHILD

Yet to all who did receive him, to those who believed in his name, he gave the right to become children of God—children born not of natural descent, nor of human decision or a husband's will, but born of God.

JOHN 1:12–13

Some of us know our origin stories. Before being adopted by a family who loved me, I was born to a single woman who was unable to raise me. Others know the family lore that although their parents were married, they came as a kind of "oops" surprise into the family! And other births are desperately longed for and carefully planned. In John's Gospel, I hear him saying that our truest identity, as children of God, doesn't depend on the story around our human birth. No, instead he insists that if we've received Christ, we have been *born* of God.

God, I thank You that my truest identity is found in You. No matter how I arrived in this world, You have called me Your daughter and have claimed me as Your own. I know that I matter to You. Amen.

GOD GRANTS HIS BELOVED SWEET REST

In vain you rise early and stay up late, toiling for food
to eat—for he grants sleep to those he loves.

PSALM 127:2

Any Christian who's had chronic difficulty sleeping has probably wrestled with the passage from Psalm 127! It can sound troubling if you read it to say, "God only gives good sleep to those He *really* loves." Problematic, right? But that's not what the psalmist is saying. Rather, the writer is describing the human impulse toward worrisome busyness and overwork. What is being communicated is that when we trust God to provide what we need, we aren't enslaved to our work. God's heart is that by trusting Him, each one of us might be liberated from the false belief that we are the gods of our lives. When we trust God, we're free to sleep—confident that God is in control.

Lord, You know my heart. You know the ways I try
to be the boss of my life. Forgive me. Teach me
how to put all of my trust in You so that
I might find freedom. Amen.

WE RELY ON THE LOVE GOD HAS FOR US

*And so we know and rely on the love God has for us. God is love.
Whoever lives in love lives in God, and God in them. This is how love
is made complete among us so that we will have confidence on the
day of judgment: In this world we are like Jesus. There is no fear in
love. But perfect love drives out fear, because fear has to do with
punishment. The one who fears is not made perfect in love.*

1 JOHN 4:16–18

Do you remember when you first came to know of God's love for you?
Maybe you learned it in Sunday school. Or maybe you had an eye-opening
moment on a youth group trip. Or maybe someone finally just shared it
with you in a way that *made sense*. When we first come to know God,
the gift of His big love for us feels amazing. But as time goes on, and we
return to the stuff of our regular lives, the freshness can wear off. But
in this little letter from John, we're reminded that God's love isn't just a
signing bonus, to get us into the club! No, the life John describes is so
much better than that: "We know and rely on the love God has for us."
Isn't that beautiful? How are you learning to *rely* on God's love?

*Father, I long to really dwell in the reality of Your love
for me. You are love and You live in me! Teach me to
stay rooted and grounded in that love. Amen.*

GOD'S UNLIKELY WAY

*If your enemy is hungry, give him food to eat; if he is thirsty,
give him water to drink. In doing this, you will heap burning
coals on his head, and the LORD will reward you.*

PROVERBS 25:21–22

If you pay attention to God's teaching throughout scripture, some of it is not surprising. That we're called to love others, show mercy, and seek justice can seem relatively intuitive. But other teachings turn the world's way of living upside down! And one of those is Jesus' teaching to love our enemies. Nothing about that is natural! The teaching is rooted here in the book of Proverbs, where the reader is exhorted to bless his enemy with food and drink. And when Paul wrote to the church in Rome, he cited this very passage in Romans 12:20. Both announce that the most wily thing we can do to spite our enemies, is actually to bless them! What can that look like in your life this week?

*Lord, I confess that Your ways are different
than my ways. Teach me what it looks like to
love my enemies in Your name. Make me
a peacemaker, in the way of Jesus. Amen.*

DWELL WITH THE LORD

Dwell in Me, and I will dwell in you. [Live in Me, and I will live in you.]. . . I am the Vine; you are the branches. Whoever lives in Me and I in him bears much (abundant) fruit. However, apart from Me [cut off from vital union with Me] you can do nothing.
JOHN 15:4–5 AMPC

I recently heard about a child whose parent was trying to explain the way that Jesus lives in our hearts. And surprising his mother, the boy barked, "Mom, don't be metaphorical!" After she stopped laughing, she realized the young theologian was correct. Because the physical body of Jesus doesn't live in our chest cavities, this is a metaphor we've been given in order to understand our relationship to Jesus. Jesus invites us to live in Him, just as He lives in us. At face value, that's a little crazy, right? Except that, by the power of God's Holy Spirit, it actually happens. This week, notice those two fundamental positions in your own life: the way you live in Christ, and the way He lives in you.

Jesus, I long to dwell with You. Thank You for the gift of Your real presence in my life! Abide with me as I abide with You. Amen.

SEEK AND YOU WILL FIND

I love those who love me, and those who seek me early and diligently shall find me. . . . For whoever finds me [Wisdom] finds life and draws forth and obtains favor from the Lord.
PROVERBS 8:17, 35 AMPC

Can you remember playing hide-and-seek when you were younger? Ideally, by the end of the game, whoever was the seeker had found all the hiders, stashed away under beds and in closets. The promise we receive in Proverbs 8 is that those who seek God will find Him. And we hear the same announcement echoed by Jesus in Matthew 7:7, "Ask and it will be given to you; seek and you will find; knock and the door will be opened to you." In both passages we get a precious glimpse into God's heart: God *longs* to be found! And He promises that those who seek Him will find Him.

Lord, I thank You for the promises I receive in Your Word. In You I find wisdom and life and favor. Thank You for the assurance that You are eager to be found! Amen.

GOD DEMONSTRATES HIS LOVE FOR US

But God demonstrates his own love for us in this:
While we were still sinners, Christ died for us.
ROMANS 5:8

As you think back on the gifts you've received throughout your lifetime, which ones have meant the most to you? For a recent birthday, a pair of friends bought me a painting they'd heard me rave about. I was thrilled to receive it! Now, if these gals had texted me to wish me a happy birthday or rung my doorbell to sing me a song, I still would have known that they loved me, right? That painting, though, was a tangible demonstration of their undeniable love for me. And Paul says that God has demonstrated His love for us by sending Jesus to die for us when we didn't deserve it. The next time you wonder if you're loved, close your eyes and think of the big price that was paid for you.

Jesus, thank You for giving Your life so that I might
live. In that demonstration, I know for certain
that You love me. Amen.

LOVE THE LORD WITH EVERYTHING IN YOU

*Hear, O Israel: The L*ORD *our God, the L*ORD *is one. Love the
L*ORD *your God with all your heart and with all your soul
and with all your strength. These commandments that
I give you today are to be on your hearts.*
DEUTERONOMY 6:4-6

Within the made-up world of *Star Trek*, the mandate not to interfere with the development of other civilizations is called the "prime directive." And in the Old Testament, God offers His people what could be called a "prime directive" to guide them in living faithfully to Him. They are to love God with everything within them. That's it. That's the big instruction. And Jesus reiterates the prime directive, adding practical application. Jesus' twofold mandate is for His followers to love God with all that they are, and to love people the way they love themselves. Were you to seize this prime directive for your life, how would you live it out this week?

*God, You have announced clearly what Your will
is for humanity and for me. Strengthen my will
to love You above all else, and teach me
how to love my neighbor. Amen.*

I WILL CALL THEM "MY PEOPLE"

*As he says in Hosea: "I will call them 'my people' who are not my
people; and I will call her 'my loved one' who is not my loved one,"
and, "In the very place where it was said to them, 'You are not
my people,' there they will be called 'children of the living God.'"*

ROMANS 9:25–26

Have you ever read the book of Hosea, in the Old Testament? It's pretty
crazy. Not only does God command Hosea to marry a prostitute named
Gomer, but they have children given absurd names like "not loved" and
"not my people." (Pretty rough, right?) But the reason God led Hosea in
this way was to show off His love. The wayward wife in this story is actually you and me. And the faithful husband who chooses us? That's God.
And by the end of the story, God has called Hosea's children "children
of the living God" (Hosea 1:10). And in his letter to the church in Rome,
God reminds the church of His unpredictable and unfathomable mercy.

*Lord, I thank You that You are merciful. And gracious.
And loving. And kind. Forgive me for my sins,
and teach me to live faithfully to You. Amen.*

WALKING THROUGH ON DRY GROUND

When Pharaoh's horses, chariots and horsemen went into the sea, the LORD brought the waters of the sea back over them, but the Israelites walked through the sea on dry ground.

EXODUS 15:19

Imagine you were hiking in the woods, following a marked trail, and came upon a river. Seeing the trail markers on the opposite side of the river, you knew that you had to cross it to reach your destination. I suspect you'd take a minute to figure out the best solution. But now imagine yourself in the same spot, but you're being chased by a bear. Who can't swim. I suspect you'd find a way to cross that river pretty quickly! When Egyptian soldiers were pursuing the Israelites as God led them out of captivity in Egypt, God parted the waters for the Israelites to walk through on dry ground. But once they'd crossed, the waters washed over their attackers. Again and again, God makes a way where it seems like there's no way.

God, Your ways are amazing. When I can't see a way forward, show me the unlikely path You've prepared for me. I put my trust in You. Amen.

SEEKING AND SAVING THE LOST

Jesus said to him, "Today salvation has come to this house,
because this man, too, is a son of Abraham. For the Son
of Man came to seek and to save the lost."
LUKE 19:9-10

When Jesus beelined toward a reputable sinner, a tax collector named Zacchaeus, the folks in his community would have been baffled! In their eyes, this guy was the *worst*. The tax collector charged them more money than he should have and pocketed the extra for himself. While we have the luxury of hindsight, and can recognize Jesus' big love for those on the margins, His care for sinners troubled a lot of religious people in the first century. So I'm wondering who those folks on the world's margins—toward whom Jesus moved—would be today. Who would Jesus head toward at your school? Who would Jesus want to share lunch with in your town? And how will Jesus reach them, today, through you?

Jesus, I confess that I feel uncomfortable around
those the Church labels as special "sinners."
Forgive me, and give me Your heart for
the lost and rejected. Amen.

GRACIOUS WORDS ARE A HONEYCOMB

Prudence is a fountain of life to the prudent, but folly brings
punishment to fools. The hearts of the wise make their mouths
prudent, and their lips promote instruction. Gracious words
are a honeycomb, sweet to the soul and healing to the bones.
PROVERBS 16:22-24

Have you ever been in the middle of speaking, and realized that you don't like the words that are coming out of your mouth? That's happened to me before. Specifically, if I'm being critical of someone else, or trying to get a laugh at someone else's expense, the Holy Spirit convicts me and I feel disappointed in the way I've wielded my tongue. Throughout the scriptures we are exhorted to use our words *well*. James even calls the tongue a rudder that can turn a huge ship! (see James 3:4) Our words have power. When we ask God for wisdom and grace, we'll use them well.

Lord, You know the way my mouth can get away
from me sometimes, revealing the condition
of my heart. Forgive me. Let me speak
only words that build up. Amen.

SEE WHAT LOVE GOD HAS FOR YOU

See what great love the Father has lavished on us, that we should be called children of God! And that is what we are! The reason the world does not know us is that it did not know him. Dear friends, now we are children of God, and what we will be has not yet been made known.

1 JOHN 3:1-2

I am both an adopted person, adopted as an infant, and also an adoptive mom, adopting my son when he was two years old. And so I feel like I know something both about being *chosen* as a child and also *choosing* to love and parent someone. When God calls you or me His child, His daughter, we are being invited to live in His house, to receive His provision, and to be enveloped by His love. There's nothing we could ever do that would cause God to reject us. This week, live into your truest identity as God's beloved daughter.

Father, I thank You that I belong to You! I am Yours and You are mine. Thank You for the gift of Your great love that does not fail. Amen.

IF GOD LOVES YOU...

"Those whom I love I rebuke and discipline. So be earnest and repent. Here I am! I stand at the door and knock. If anyone hears my voice and opens the door, I will come in and eat with that person, and they with me. To the one who is victorious, I will give the right to sit with me on my throne, just as I was victorious and sat down with my Father on his throne."

REVELATION 3:19–21

Do you live in a home where your parents discipline you when you behave badly? Maybe they take away your phone privileges if they catch you using it after hours. Or you might get grounded if you come in after curfew. While being disciplined typically isn't any fun, you probably understand why parents need to do it, right? Because they want you to flourish and thrive, they teach you to make better choices by disciplining you. And the scripture says that God rebukes and disciplines the ones He loves. God doesn't just let us behave however we choose. Because God loves us, God is eager to discipline us when we repent.

Lord, You know the ways I've sinned. And although I don't always like the consequences, I welcome Your discipline that brings new life. Transform my heart so that I might be more like You. Amen.

YOU ARE CHRIST'S BODY

*Now you [collectively] are Christ's body and [individually]
you are members of it, each part severally and distinct
[each with his own place and function].*
1 CORINTHIANS 12:27 AMPC

When the apostle Paul wrote to the Corinthian church, he told them that they were all members of Christ's body. And what he's saying, to them and to you, is this: *you matter.* You already matter to God because you're His beloved daughter. But you also matter because you have been given gifts to be used to build God's kingdom. Maybe you're the arms that rock babies or dig wells. Or perhaps you're the eyes that notice those who are hurting. Or it might be that you're the ears who pay attention and listen well to others. Or you might be the tongue who blesses others with your speech. The body of Christ needs you to use your gift!

*Lord, I do thank You that You've given me gifts and
talents meant to glorify You. I offer You all that
I am, and ask You to use me so that You
might be known and loved. Amen.*

BUILD YOURSELF UP

But you, dear friends, by building yourselves up in your most holy faith and praying in the Holy Spirit, keep yourselves in God's love as you wait for the mercy of our Lord Jesus Christ to bring you to eternal life.
JUDE 1:20–21

Where I live, I'm always seeing people working out. Two blocks west of me, at Crossfit, folks are lifting huge metal objects, tossing massive balls, and running up and down the street. Four blocks south of me, at the YMCA, people are swimming, running, and lifting to stay in shape. And the same way we invest in our physical health, we're invited to invest in our spiritual health. When we pray in the Holy Spirit, we become rooted and grounded in God's love. When we pray, we *build spiritual muscle* that sustains us until we meet the Lord in heaven.

God, I give You thanks for Your Word. Send Your Holy Spirit to help me as I pray. And when I pray, I trust that You are grounding me in the reality of Your love. Amen.

I WILL HELP YOU AND TEACH YOU WHAT TO SAY

"Pardon your servant, Lord. I have never been eloquent, neither in the past nor since you have spoken to your servant. I am slow of speech and tongue." The LORD said to him, "Who gave human beings their mouths? Who makes them deaf or mute? Who gives them sight or makes them blind? Is it not I, the LORD? Now go; I will help you speak and will teach you what to say."

EXODUS 4:10-12

When people are surveyed about the fears that move them most, the number one human fear mentioned is a fear of public speaking! That's what Moses felt when God sent Moses to be His spokesperson in the world. Moses protested, claiming, "I am slow of speech and tongue." As you might imagine, the Lord wasn't having it. Instead, God promised to help Moses speak and to teach him what to say. (Not a bad speech coach, right?!) When God asks you to speak—sharing the Gospel with a friend, encouraging someone, or standing up for injustice the way Moses did—know that God will be your helper!

Lord, I long to be faithful in speaking words of life on Your behalf. So I ask You to be my helper and teach me what to say! Amen.

I AM HE

The woman said to Him, I know that Messiah is coming,
He Who is called the Christ (the Anointed One); and when He
arrives, He will tell us everything we need to know and make it
clear to us. Jesus said to her, I Who now speak with you am He.
JOHN 4:25–26 AMPC

In this fabulous conversation between Jesus and a Samaritan woman at a well, she doesn't quite realize who she's speaking with. We know this because she tells Jesus that the Messiah is coming. She's eager to meet the One called "the Christ," because she knows He'll tell them all they need to know. By the end of their wonderful exchange—that I hope you'll dig into in the fourth chapter of John's Gospel—she has discovered the One who *is* the Christ! And because it's been made clear to her, she runs off to tell everyone else that the Messiah has come.

Jesus, sometimes I'm blinded like this woman. I don't
see You for who You really are. By the power of Your
Spirit, remove the blinders from my heart so that I can
see You clearly and share You with others. Amen.

GOD'S DWELLING PLACE IS NOW AMONG THE PEOPLE

And I heard a loud voice from the throne saying, "Look! God's dwelling place is now among the people, and he will dwell with them. They will be his people, and God himself will be with them and be their God. 'He will wipe every tear from their eyes. There will be no more death' or mourning or crying or pain, for the old order of things has passed away."

REVELATION 21:3-4

In the last book of the Bible, called Revelation, we get a little glimpse into heaven! It's not a clear picture, because some of it can be tricky to understand, but we can glean the essence of God's heart for the people He loves. Specifically, God promises to dwell among His people. And when that day comes, it will be so good that there will be no more crying. Pretty cool, right? We have had a taste of God living among us, in the person of Jesus, and one day we'll know fully what it means to dwell in God's presence.

God, I love that this is Your heart for humanity. Thank You that You long to be with us and to grant us the peace and healing of brokenness for which we long. Come, Lord Jesus! Amen.

I WILL SEE GOD'S GOODNESS IN THE LAND OF THE LIVING

I remain confident of this: I will see the goodness of the LORD
in the land of the living. Wait for the LORD; be strong
and take heart and wait for the LORD.

PSALM 27:13–14

In Psalm 27, the writer is honest about his struggles and fears. And yet again and again the psalmist trusts in God's reliable love. And what's particularly unique about this prayer is that the psalmist isn't longing for peace in a life after this one. No, instead the writer announces, "I will see the goodness of the LORD in the land of the living." That basically means, "God, I'm counting on You to help me while I'm living, not after I've died!" It's a pretty bold thing to ask, isn't it? And the psalmist encourages his audience, "Wait for the LORD; be strong and take courage and wait for the LORD."

God, I trust that You are with me and You are for
me. And with the psalmist I beg You to answer
my prayer so that I might see Your goodness
on this side of heaven. Amen.

HAVING ASSURANCE ABOUT WHAT WE DO NOT SEE

Now faith is confidence in what we hope for and assurance about
what we do not see. This is what the ancients were commended for.
By faith we understand that the universe was formed at God's
command, so that what is seen was not made out of what was visible.
HEBREWS 11:1–3

If your dad says you're having chocolate chip cookies for dessert after dinner, and you smell them baking in the oven, it's pretty easy to believe that you'll receive what he's promised. Or if your mom says that she's bought you a new bike, and you see one locked to the backyard fence, you're likely to believe her! It's easy enough to trust in what we can see, hear, taste, touch, and smell! But what about the things we've been promised that we can't see? The author of Hebrews names real faith as having confidence in what we hope for but can't yet see. Are you willing to exercise this kind of faith in God?

God, it's easy to trust You for what I can already see.
But I'm asking You to give me big faith, the kind
that trusts You for what cannot yet be
seen. For Your sake, amen.

THE LORD REMEMBERS US

The LORD remembers us and will bless us: He will bless his
people Israel, he will bless the house of Aaron, he will
bless those who fear the LORD—small and great alike.
PSALM 115:12-13

Have you ever run into someone who didn't quite remember who you were? Maybe it was an old family friend who hadn't seen you since you were a baby. Or perhaps it was a nursery school teacher who couldn't quite place you. The psalmist assures us that the Lord never forgets us. In fact, God holds each of us in His heart. And the psalmist also promises that God will bless His people who fear Him, both small and great alike. As you close your eyes and picture the loving heart of God, ask God to show you nestled in there! You are loved. You are remembered. You matter.

God, You know that sometimes I feel insignificant,
as though no one cares for me. Thank You for
this promise from Your Word that I matter to
You and You hold me in Your heart. Amen.

A DEEP LONGING FOR MORE

Instead, they were longing for a better country—a heavenly one. Therefore God is not ashamed to be called their God, for he has prepared a city for them.

HEBREWS 11:16

To encourage Christians seeking to live faithfully to Jesus, the author of Hebrews reminds us of the faithful ones who preceded us: Abraham, Isaac, Jacob, and Sarah. Each one trusted God when they couldn't quite yet see how the rest of the story would unfold. And each one was longing for something more than they'd experienced: a heavenly home where God would be in charge. And the writer promises that, in fact, God has prepared a city to receive those who are faithful. Today we continue to long for that perfect city where God will make everything right.

Lord, like Your faithful people who've gone before me, I am longing for a perfect world. When I see the brokenness around me, my soul thirsts to be with You. Today, I depend on You for strength, and I look forward to what will come! Amen.

A DEEP LONGING FOR MORE

In the year that King Uzziah died, I saw the Lord, high and exalted, seated on a throne; and the train of his robe filled the temple. Above him were seraphim, each with six wings: With two wings they covered their faces, with two they covered their feet, and with two they were flying. And they were calling to one another: "Holy, holy, holy is the LORD Almighty; the whole earth is full of his glory."
ISAIAH 6:1–3

Did you know that you were made to praise God? I'll bet you've done it with your voice on Sunday mornings. Or maybe you rock out to worship music in your bedroom. Or perhaps you praise God by writing out prayers. It's what you were created to do. Jesus says that if we keep our mouths shut, the way religious folk wanted to silence His disciples, the stones would cry out! (see Luke 19:40). And Isaiah describes heavenly beings who worship God day and night singing, "Holy, holy, holy!" When you praise God, you join this chorus that's been heard throughout the ages.

God, I believe that You are worthy of all praise and glory. Let my heart and lips and voice praise You, because You alone are worthy. Amen.

BE STRONG, BE ALERT, BE COURAGEOUS

Be strong, alert, and courageous, all you people of the land,
says the Lord, and work! For I am with you, says the Lord of
hosts. . . . My Spirit stands and abides in the midst of you; fear not.
HAGGAI 2:4–5 AMPC

Throughout the scriptures, when life gets really tough for God's people—when it's scary, when it's dangerous, when it's uncertain—God promises to be with us. He doesn't just look on from a distance, but God is actually *with us* in our toughest times. And because we have the promise that God's Spirit abides with us, we can be strong. We can be alert. We can be courageous. Whether we have to be brave to say something hard to an adult, or if we can't quite figure out how we'll pay for college, or if we need to stand up for someone who's vulnerable, God promises to be our helper.

God, when times are good I can forget to depend
on You. But when things get tight, when I can't manage
on my own, I thank You that You promise to be
with me. Today, my courage and strength
come from You! Amen.

DO YOU JUDGE AND DO THE SAME THINGS?

*So when you, a mere human being, pass judgment on them and yet
do the same things, do you think you will escape God's judgment?
Or do you show contempt for the riches of his kindness,
forbearance and patience, not realizing that God's
kindness is intended to lead you to repentance?*

ROMANS 2:3-4

Not long after I mutter crabby words about the way someone is driving in front of me, I'll get in a pickle and do something similar. Or maybe I'll quietly judge a friend for talking trash about someone else, but then I'll hear myself say something that's not entirely kind. So not only am I judging others, but I am literally judging them for the exact things I'm doing myself. Often what we find most intolerable in others are the ways they reflect something of our own sin and brokenness! But Paul directs our gaze from ourselves *and* others and toward the One who loves us from "the riches of his kindness." That is what can change our hearts!

*Lord, You know the condition of my heart.
Forgive me when I judge others, and fill me
with Your own kindness, forbearance,
and patience, for Your glory. Amen.*

I AM WITH YOU

"Before I formed you in the womb I knew you, before you were born I set you apart; I appointed you as a prophet to the nations." "Alas, Sovereign LORD," I said, "I do not know how to speak; I am too young." But the LORD said to me, "Do not say, 'I am too young.' You must go to everyone I send you to and say whatever I command you. Do not be afraid of them, for I am with you and will rescue you," declares the LORD.

JEREMIAH 1:4-8

As we eavesdrop on God's calling of Jeremiah, we hear big themes that are also woven throughout other parts of scripture. God's announcement that He formed Jeremiah in his mother's womb resonates with what we learn about God in Psalm 139. And Jeremiah's resistance to God's call, expressing his sense of inadequacy at being so young, sounds like Moses and many others God sends. (Maybe he was a teenager!) Bottom line, though, is that God promises to be with Jeremiah and to help him. And that is God's promise to you as well.

Lord, I want to say yes to You when You call! Give me the courage and faith to respond in obedience when You call me to serve You. Amen.

JESUS' PRAYER FOR HIS DISCIPLES

"My prayer is not that you take them out of the world but that you protect them from the evil one. They are not of the world, even as I am not of it. Sanctify them by the truth; your word is truth. As you sent me into the world, I have sent them into the world. For them I sanctify myself, that they too may be truly sanctified."

JOHN 17:15–19

At the end of Jesus' earthly ministry, we get a beautiful rare peek into His prayer life. We get to hear Jesus speaking to His Father! And His prayer for His friends, His disciples, before He leaves them is a powerful one: "My prayer is not that you take them out of the world but that you protect them from the evil one." When we face challenges, a lot of us wonder why God didn't just spare us from them in the first place. That's a legit question, right? And it makes sense that we'd rather avoid what's hard. But Jesus' prayer reminds us that although we encounter difficulties, God is faithful to protect us from the enemy. This week, as you face what you'd rather not, join Jesus' prayer by asking God to protect you from the evil one.

God, You already know the challenges I am facing
and will face. So today I pray with Jesus, asking
You to protect me from the enemy of my soul. Amen.

CAN WORDS BE ALIVE?

For the word of God is alive and active. Sharper than any double-edged sword, it penetrates even to dividing soul and spirit, joints and marrow; it judges the thoughts and attitudes of the heart. Nothing in all creation is hidden from God's sight. Everything is uncovered and laid bare before the eyes of him to whom we must give account.

HEBREWS 4:12-13

Sometimes in our culture you might hear people making reference to the Bible as an ancient out-of-date book with little relevance to our modern lives. And while the Bible does reflect the culture and time in which it was written, nothing could be further from the truth! The author of Hebrews reminds us that God's Word isn't a stagnant document, like a textbook or instruction manual might be. God's Word is alive! Using beautiful, poetic language, the writer claims that God's Word is "sharper than any double-edged sword" because it has the ability to get inside us. It opens our eyes and ears to what's most true about God, about ourselves, and about others.

God, today I submit myself to the power of Your holy Word. Show me what I need to discover, and help me be faithful as I respond. Amen.

MY EARNEST PRAYER WENT OUT TO YOU

*"I sank beneath the waves, and the waters closed over me.
Seaweed wrapped itself around my head. . . . As my life
was slipping away, I remembered the LORD. And my
earnest prayer went out to you in your holy Temple."*
JONAH 2:5, 7 NLT

Are you familiar with the story of Jonah? God charged Jonah to go minister to the people of Nineveh, but Jonah was not having it. When he attempted to flee, bringing danger to everyone on the boat he was in, he got thrown overboard and swallowed by a huge fish. (Bad day, right?) That's when Jonah made the first good decision he'd made in a while: he prayed to God. With seaweed wrapped around his head, on the edge of death by digestion, Jonah remembered the Lord and asked for help. And guess what? *God helped.* It's what God loves to do. In any situation in which you ever find yourself, God longs to hear your prayer and be your helper.

*Lord, I thank You that there is no situation I could
choose, or to which I could be subjected, in which
You would not hear my prayer. Thank You for
being my faithful deliverer. Amen.*

118

IN YOUR ANGER, DO NOT SIN

Therefore each of you must put off falsehood and speak truthfully
to your neighbor, for we are all members of one body. "In your
anger do not sin": Do not let the sun go down while you
are still angry, and do not give the devil a foothold.
EPHESIANS 4:25–27

Do you think Christians are allowed to be angry? Some families communicate to children that they shouldn't be angry. That instead of being angry, they need to smile and pretend everything's okay. But that's not biblical. In the Old Testament we meet a God who was angry at injustice because He loved the people who were being harmed by it! When Paul says, "In your anger do not sin," he's not saying don't be angry. When children are harmed, or people are enslaved, or elder folks are neglected, we *should* be angry! But Paul teaches that we can be angry without *sinning*. We can use the righteous energy of our anger to effect change without sinning against God or others.

God, I praise You for being a God of justice. Teach me
what it means to share Your righteous anger and to
be faithful in my response as Your disciple. Amen.

I WILL BE HIS FATHER

"He is the one who will build a house for my Name,
and I will establish the throne of his kingdom forever.
I will be his father, and he will be my son."

2 SAMUEL 7:13–14

What would you think if I told you that Jesus was not His Father's first son on earth? Because the Father and Son have existed together since before time, Jesus does have bragging rights as the firstborn. But before Jesus was born to a woman, there was another human being that God called "son." When God called David, through the voice of his prophet Samuel, he announced, "I will be his father, and he will be my son." So when David ruled over Israel, he didn't do it solely on his own authority. In a very particular way, he represented the God of Israel. While that's not quite how politics work today, the fact that God has called you His daughter means that you are God's representative in the world, as a builder and bearer of His kingdom.

God, thank You for calling me Your own. I offer myself
as Your servant and welcome You to guide me by Your
Holy Spirit as I represent You on earth. Amen.

THE MISSION OF GOD'S SERVANT

The Spirit of the Sovereign LORD is on me, because the LORD has anointed me to proclaim good news to the poor. He has sent me to bind up the brokenhearted, to proclaim freedom for the captives and release from darkness for the prisoners, to proclaim the year of the LORD's favor and the day of vengeance of our God, to comfort all who mourn, and provide for those who grieve in Zion.

ISAIAH 61:1-3

In the third Gospel, Luke describes what was kind of like Jesus' inaugural address at the beginning of His earthly ministry. When He stood in the synagogue to read, the scroll of Isaiah was handed to Him. Unrolling it, He found the part that was about Him! Centuries earlier, God had promised that His servant would bring good news to the poor and freedom for captives. And when Jesus read those words—the same ones that had been read in the synagogue in Nazareth for centuries—they finally came alive. They were being realized in the person of Jesus!

Lord, thank You for sending Your servant Jesus to redeem the world. In Him, the poor and brokenhearted receive good news! And in Him, I receive good news! Amen.

GOOD RELIGION AND BAD RELIGION

*Those who consider themselves religious and yet do not keep a
tight rein on their tongues deceive themselves, and their religion is
worthless. Religion that God our Father accepts as pure and faultless
is this: to look after orphans and widows in their distress and
to keep oneself from being polluted by the world.*

JAMES 1:26–27

These days, the words *religion* and *religious* have really taken a beating. Even Christians who love and follow Jesus often want to separate themselves from people who are "religious." But in the first century, religion didn't have some of the negative connotation it does today. Still, James wanted to be particular about the kind of religion that honors God. The worthless kind, he writes, is practiced by those who don't keep a tight rein on their tongues. And these ones might not even realize that they're deceived! The real deal, though? The kind of "religion" that delights the heart of God? It's the same today as it was back then: caring for widows and orphans, and keeping one's self pure. That, James claims, is what pleases God.

*Father, I long to be faithful to You. Show me, in my
life, how I can care for those You love who suffer
with desperate needs. And help my heart
remain pure, for Your sake. Amen.*

RULING OVER THE EARTH

Then God said, "Let us make mankind in our image, in our likeness,
so that they may rule over the fish in the sea and the birds in the
sky, over the livestock and all the wild animals, and over
all the creatures that move along the ground."

GENESIS 1:26

When God created humankind in His image, He announced that they—that we!—would rule over all the critters on the planet. Then, after charging them to multiply, God gave human beings charge over everything that grows on the earth as well. Pretty big job, right? Some scholars even argue that this—stewardship of what God has made—is what it means to reflect the image of God. The charge that was given to Adam and Eve is the same one for which we're responsible today. And in a world in which God's resources are increasingly abused, it's become important to find ways to be faithful stewards of God's creation in what we buy, what we eat, and how we live.

Good Creator, thank You for creating and sustaining
us with such abundant resources. You have been
a faithful provider. Show me how I can honor
and protect Your creation. Amen.

123

DEFEATING THE DEVIL

*Jesus, full of the Holy Spirit, left the Jordan and was led by the Spirit
into the wilderness, where for forty days he was tempted by the devil.
He ate nothing during those days, and at the end of them he
was hungry. The devil said to him, "If you are the Son of
God, tell this stone to become bread." Jesus answered,
"It is written: Man shall not live on bread alone."*

LUKE 4:1–4

Have you ever seen an animated cartoon where someone has a devil
on one shoulder, speaking temptation into one ear, and an angel on the
other shoulder, giving her wise counsel in the other other? Those kind of
silly portrayals don't do justice to the cunning of our enemy! When Luke
gives us a peek into Jesus' encounter with Satan, Jesus models for us
how to defeat that snake. When Satan tempts Him, Jesus always answers
the temptation with scripture. He doesn't count on good intentions or
even willpower—though He no doubt possessed both. When He was at
His weakest, physically, Jesus drew power from what God provided.

*Lord, You know the ways I'm tempted. And thank You
for the assurance that, like Jesus, I can also resist
temptation by relying on Your Holy Word. Amen.*

WHAT I'VE LEARNED I'VE MADE KNOWN

"You are my friends if you do what I command. I no longer call you servants, because a servant does not know his master's business. Instead, I have called you friends, for everything that I learned from my Father I have made known to you."

JOHN 15:14–15

When Jesus knew His earthly life was drawing to a close, He gathered His friends to equip them so they'd know how to live in His absence. And what makes them *friends*, Jesus implies here, is that whatever Jesus learned from His Father, He shared with them. To my ear, that's a pretty cool definition of friendship! Are you sharing with your friends what it is that you're learning from the Father? Maybe you have a chance to share that kind of thing in a small group setting. Or maybe it's something you and your friend discuss on the way to school. As the Father shows Himself to you, be sure to share it with your friends.

Jesus, I thank You for the love You had for Your friends. You lived faithfully among them, and I long to live faithfully among the friends in my life. Amen.

STAYING ON THE RIGHT PATH

How can a young person stay on the path of purity? By living according to your word. I seek you with all my heart; do not let me stray from your commands. I have hidden your word in my heart that I might not sin against you.

PSALM 119:9–11

You might remember that Psalm 119 describes and celebrates living a life that God orders and blesses. The longest psalm in the Bible, every single verse refers in some way to living life well, according to God's design. We discover that we experience authentic life when we submit ourselves to be guided by God's Word so that we can walk in His way. We find that sacred route by clinging to what the psalmist describes as the "path of purity," "your word," and "your commands." Is there a way, today, in which you've strayed from the path you know God has prepared for you? How is God inviting you to return to the way?

Lord, thank You that You are faithful to lead me in the paths of life. This week, open my eyes to the way You have prepared for me. Amen.

AN UNLIKELY POWER

But he said to me, "My grace is sufficient for you, for my power is made perfect in weakness." Therefore I will boast all the more gladly about my weaknesses, so that Christ's power may rest on me. That is why, for Christ's sake, I delight in weaknesses, in insults, in hardships, in persecutions, in difficulties. For when I am weak, then I am strong.
2 CORINTHIANS 12:9-10

In this world, the strongest survive. You've seen it on YouTube videos or Animal Planet where animals must fight to survive. You've seen it on reality TV shows where everyone's competing to win a prize. You've probably even seen it in your high school! No one is aspiring to be *weak.* Except. . .Christians are. When Jesus first gave up His heavenly privileges and then went on to give up His human life for us, He turned the tables upside down! In one of the profound mysteries of the Gospel, we are strongest—through God's strength inside us—when we are weak.

Lord, I don't completely understand how You work.
And yet I do believe that Your strength can be seen
most clearly through my weaknesses. May Your
strength be seen in me! Amen.

A SHEPHERD WHO IS GOOD

The LORD is my shepherd, I lack nothing. He makes me lie down in green pastures, he leads me beside quiet waters, he refreshes my soul. He guides me along the right paths for his name's sake. Even though I walk through the darkest valley, I will fear no evil, for you are with me; your rod and your staff, they comfort me.

PSALM 23:1–4

In one of the most undeniably popular psalms, the writer identifies God as a shepherd. If you don't live in an agrarian culture, you might not know exactly what that means! The shepherd makes sure that the sheep get what they most need: safety, rest, food, and drink. When a sheep wanders off, the shepherd uses his rod and staff—often used to discipline the sheep—to drive any wayward sheep back to the herd. The psalmist has known God to be One who makes sure our needs are met. One who gives us rest. One who feeds. One who protects.

*God, I long to know You as the Shepherd who is good.
You know the ways I'm tempted to wander away.
Hold me close to Your side so that I can
find my life in You. Amen.*

HONOR OTHERS ABOVE YOURSELF

Love must be sincere. Hate what is evil; cling to what is good.
Be devoted to one another in love. Honor one
another above yourselves.

ROMANS 12:9-10

No doubt knit into our wiring as an important survival skill, the desires for satisfaction and pleasure lead us awry when we begin to think only of our own needs and desires. And as the apostle Paul coaches the believers in Rome how to live together as the body of Christ, he reminds them to honor others above themselves. If we think of honoring our parents, or grandparents, or other adult authority figures in our lives, it makes sense. Of course we'll honor them over ourselves. But what about when it's a little cousin who drives us crazy? Or the kid at school who eats lunch alone? Ask God to show you what it means to honor others above yourself.

Lord, teach me Your ways. I long to think of others
more than I think of myself, and to serve them
more than I serve myself. Set me free so
that I might love like You love. Amen.

THE GLORIOUS SILENCE OF GOD

The Lord your God is in the midst of you, a Mighty One, a Savior
[Who saves]! He will rejoice over you with joy; He will rest [in silent
satisfaction] and in His love He will be silent and make no mention [of
past sins, or even recall them]; He will exult over you with singing.
ZEPHANIAH 3:17 AMPC

It's a gift to hear from God. Maybe we've been begging God for an answer and, as we're reading scripture, the answer shows up plain as day. Or perhaps God speaks to us through the lips of someone we trust, like a parent or a leader at church. We are blessed when we hear God's voice. So the exhortation from Zephaniah about God's silence is a bit of a curve ball, right? But the silence he describes is a holy silence. Zephaniah says that instead of reminding us of our sins, God makes no mention of them. In fact, He can't even remember them!

Lord, when I hear a nagging voice reminding me of
the sins You've already forgiven, I know that that
voice is not Yours. You do not condemn,
but You rejoice over me! Amen.

THIS IS THE MEASURE OF LOVE

This is how we know what love is: Jesus Christ laid down his life for us. And we ought to lay down our lives for our brothers and sisters. If anyone has material possessions and sees a brother or sister in need but has no pity on them, how can the love of God be in that person? Dear children, let us not love with words or speech but with actions and in truth.

1 JOHN 3:16–18

If you want to know how many slices of cheese are in a package, you can count them. But love? That's a little trickier to measure, isn't it? And yet John actually offers a way. The measure of love, he claims, is the way Jesus loved us. He laid down His life for us (#biglove!), and when we love others well, we lay down our lives for them. He even offers a clear example of self-giving love: when people lack what they need materially—food, clothing, housing—we care for them by giving from what we have.

I want to really love others by sharing with them from all You've given to me. Teach me to love sacrificially as You did. Amen.

A REFUGE IN TIMES OF TROUBLE

The LORD is good, a refuge in times of trouble.
He cares for those who trust in him.
NAHUM 1:7

When our lives are going well—when we're getting good grades, when we're having fun with our friends, when we're healthy and strong—it can be tempting to put our faith in God on autopilot. Go to church? Check the box. Read a daily devotion? Check. And then when life takes a twist we didn't see coming, when we experience loss or hardship, we're suddenly more motivated to draw near to God. Graciously, when we move toward God, God moves toward us. And God's Word promises us that the Lord is a refuge in times of trouble. When we put our trust in God, God cares for us. When have you experienced God's care in hardship?

Lord, thank You that You are good. You are a mighty
fortress and refuge in times of trouble. I see how
You've cared for me in the past, and I seek
refuge in Your love today. Amen.

I AM THE LIGHT OF THE WORLD

Then Jesus again spoke to them, saying, "I am the Light of the world; he who follows Me will not walk in the darkness, but will have the Light of life."

JOHN 8:12 NASB

A lot of us who live "on the grid" and have constant access to conveniences like electric lights in our homes, streetlights, and cell phones may not have experienced utter darkness. But if you get far away from civilization, camping outside on a moonless night, you will discover what darkness really is! When Jesus identified Himself to those who were curious about Him, He claimed to be the Light of the world. And though it's not obvious to the modern ear, that was actually a royal designation in the ancient world: the "light of the world" was how a king would be described! And indeed, Jesus is the King who brings light into the darkness of our lives when we follow Him.

Jesus, as I follow Your light, You lead me into life. Thank You for who You are. Open my eyes so that I can see You plainly. Amen.

WHAT DO YOU WANT JESUS TO DO FOR YOU?

*Throwing his cloak aside, he jumped to his feet and came to Jesus.
"What do you want me to do for you?" Jesus asked him. The blind
man said, "Rabbi, I want to see." "Go," said Jesus, "your faith
has healed you." Immediately he received his sight
and followed Jesus along the road.*

MARK 10:50-52

Jesus' question to a man who was blind seems a little unnecessary, doesn't it? Like if you made an appointment with a specialist and walked into his office with a fork sticking out of your foot, the reason for your visit would be apparent. But there's clearly something that happens when we're able to speak our need to Jesus. *"Rabbi, I want to see." "Lord, save me." "Jesus, my heart is in need of healing."* When we bring our requests to Jesus, we participate in what He longs to do in our lives by demonstrating faith in who He is.

*Jesus, You've made Yourself known as the Great
Physician. I believe that You healed many and
that You can heal me. So I name what I
need, and I put my faith in You. Amen.*

134

LOVE IS AS STRONG AS DEATH

Place me like a seal over your heart, like a seal on your arm;
for love is as strong as death, its jealousy unyielding as the
grave. It burns like blazing fire, like a mighty flame.
SONG OF SONGS 8:6

One of the driving factors in human behavior is an anxiety that some of us think about often and others avoid thinking about altogether: our fear of death. Even if it's not consciously on our mind, this innate instinct protects us from harm because it quietly motivates us to avoid dangerous or threatening situations. In a beautiful, poetic love song that we read in the Old Testament, Song of Songs, the writer claims that there is a force that is as strong as death: *love.* I've seen it in my relationships and I also see it in the person of Jesus. His great love for us defeated the power of the grave.

Jesus, I praise You that You have defeated death once
and for all. Thank You for releasing me from death's
grip once and for all. Teach me how to live as
one who does NOT live in fear. Amen.

SUFFERING LEADS TO HOPE

Not only so, but we also glory in our sufferings, because we know that suffering produces perseverance; perseverance, character; and character, hope. And hope does not put us to shame, because God's love has been poured out into our hearts through the Holy Spirit, who has been given to us.

ROMANS 5:3–5

When we're suffering, it's hard to see much else. If we're experiencing depression, if we've lost a loved one, or if we're enduring physical pain, it's natural that we would be consumed with our suffering. In his letter to the church in Rome, Paul reminds those who might be suffering that, for believers, suffering is not an end in itself. Rather, when we trust in Jesus, suffering can produce perseverance, or *grit*. And that perseverance is the way we develop character. And that character produces hope! If you are suffering today, know that God is with you. If you allow it, one day it can bear fruit in your life.

Lord, You know I wouldn't choose the suffering I've faced. But I do trust that You can redeem it for Your purposes and my good. Come, Lord Jesus! Amen.

WE BELONG TO GOD

*For none of us lives for ourselves alone, and none of us dies for
ourselves alone. If we live, we live for the Lord; and if we die, we die
for the Lord. So, whether we live or die, we belong to the Lord. For this
very reason, Christ died and returned to life so that he might
be the Lord of both the dead and the living.*

ROMANS 14:7–9

Have you ever known anyone who's died? Some, trusting in God's goodness, will calmly slide gently into God's loving arms. And others, for any host of reasons, will be afraid and resist death until their last breath. What I've seen in those who exit this world gently as their earthly lives draw to a close, to be received by God into the next, is that they trust in God's loving care. They reflect this attitude of Paul: "if we live, we live for the Lord; and if we die, we die for the Lord." Doesn't that sound like the most wonderful freedom? Beloved, know that in life and in death you belong to God.

*God, I thank You for the solid assurance that You are
the Lord of all. I believe that whether I live or
whether I die, I belong to You! Amen.*

THE PLANS GOD HAS FOR YOU

"I know what I'm doing. I have it all planned out—plans to take care of you, not abandon you, plans to give you the future you hope for."
JEREMIAH 29:11 MSG

After God's people have been carried off into exile in Babylon, they're reeling and confused. And God gives them unlikely instructions. Rather than commanding them to sneak away in the dead of night and return home, He tells them to plant themselves in this new land. He instructs them to marry and have families. And God promises to come to them after *seventy years* to make good on His promise to help them return home. (Yikes!) In the midst of what feels like a cruel punishment, God reassures His beloved people that He's got their back. In fact, He has good intentions and plans for their lives. Are you able to believe, today, that God has good in store for you?

Lord, it's not always obvious, from my circumstances,
that You have good in store for me. But I do trust
that You care for me and will never abandon
me. I put my hope in You! Amen.

A DIFFERENT KIND OF PEACE

"Peace I leave with you; My [own] peace I now give and bequeath to you. Not as the world gives do I give to you. Do not let your hearts be troubled, neither let them be afraid. [Stop allowing yourselves to be agitated and disturbed; and do not permit yourselves to be fearful and intimidated and cowardly and unsettled.]"

JOHN 14:27 AMPC

In the 1960s and 1970s groovy hippies dressed in cut-off blue jeans and tie-dye T-shirts, who wanted peace and not war, were waving the two-fingered peace sign. In the ancient world, though, and especially in the Jewish context, "peace" meant much more than the absence of war. In Hebrew, the word *shalom*—that's often translated as "peace"—signaled a holistic comprehensive sense of well-being. And this is the kind of peace Jesus is offering those who trust Him. And He's clear: it means something different than the world's definition of *peace*. When we purpose to trust God with all that we are, offering Him our whole hearts, God grants us a peace that passes understanding.

Jesus, I long to experience the peace You give. Fill my heart with Your Spirit so that I might receive all You offer. Quiet my troubled heart as I trust in You. Amen.

COMPETE TO GET THE PRIZE

Do you not know that in a race all the runners run, but only one gets the prize? Run in such a way as to get the prize. Everyone who competes in the games goes into strict training. They do it to get a crown that will not last, but we do it to get a crown that will last forever.

1 CORINTHIANS 9:24–25

Have you ever had a coach who really pushed you hard? Have you ever given everything you had during sprints, weight training, or drills? That's the kind of training that Paul is recommending for early Christians. No, they didn't have to do cardio, but he was exhorting them to *strive for excellence*. A lot of us give 110 percent to our athletic teams, our schoolwork, or even our part-time jobs, and Paul is saying that we're to do the same as followers of Christ. The reason, says Paul? It's because it's an investment that lasts.

Jesus, I hear You calling me to excellence in my relationship with You and in the way I live out my faith in the world. So I submit myself to You as my master trainer. Teach me Your ways so that I might glorify You in all I do. Amen.

HE PUTS VICTIMS BACK ON THEIR FEET

GOD makes everything come out right; he puts victims back on their feet. . . . GOD's love, though, is ever and always, eternally present to all who fear him, making everything right for them and their children as they follow his Covenant ways and remember to do whatever he said.

PSALM 103:6, 17–19 MSG

Are you familiar with this paraphrase from the Bible called *The Message*? Author and pastor Eugene Peterson, a scholar versed in the ancient biblical languages, has listened closely to the original texts and translated, or paraphrased, the way they'd sound today. And the phrasing in this psalm that lights my fire is, "he puts victims back on their feet." Other translations say something along the lines of God working "justice for all the oppressed" (Psalm 103:6). But I'm really moved by this tender image of God caring for victims and putting them back on their feet. This is the intimate love God has for us.

Lord, I thank You that You are a God who loves justice and righteousness. Let Your justice prevail on earth. I also love that You care passionately for those who are victims of injustice. Shower them with Your love, and put them back on their feet. Amen.

THE PROOF IS IN THE PUDDING

Dear friends, let us love one another, for love comes from
God. Everyone who loves has been born of God and knows God.
Whoever does not love does not know God, because God is love.
This is how God showed his love among us: He sent his one
and only Son into the world that we might live through him.

1 JOHN 4:7-9

Have you ever heard someone say "The proof is in the pudding"? It's a way of saying that if you really want to know what's in something, you need to eat it. If you really want to know if your friend's mom's chocolate chip cookies are better than your mom's cookies, you have to taste them. You get the yummy idea. John knows that the proof is in the pudding: If you've been born of God and know God, you will *love others*. Because God is love, it's that simple. But don't worry about using the foolproof pudding test to judge others. The big question is, "If God is love, are you loving others?"

God, I thank You that You are love. Thank You
for taking on human flesh, in the person of
Jesus, to show us what Your love is like.
Teach me to love like Him. Amen.

A GENTLE ANSWER MAKES THINGS BETTER

A gentle answer turns away wrath, but a harsh word stirs up anger.
The tongue of the wise adorns knowledge, but the mouth of the fool
gushes folly. The eyes of the LORD are everywhere, keeping watch
on the wicked and the good. The soothing tongue is a tree
of life, but a perverse tongue crushes the spirit.

PROVERBS 15:1–4

If your siblings or parents were asked if you have a fiery temper and a loose tongue or whether you're a more even-keeled girl who speaks words that are gentle and kind, how would they answer? (I'll bet you don't even have to ask them to know the answer to this one! Lol.) The words we use are powerful, and when we use ones that are harsh, we actually cause harm to people and relationships. The wise young woman speaks soothing words that give life to others. Be that girl!

Lord, You know how I'm built. You also know that I do
want to honor You with the words that come out of my
mouth. Send Your Spirit to guide me so that I might
speak words of wisdom that come from You. Amen.

BREAD THAT SATISFIES

*"Your ancestors ate manna in the wilderness, but they all died.
Anyone who eats the bread from heaven, however, will never die. I am
the living bread that came down from heaven. Anyone who eats this
bread will live forever; and this bread, which I will offer. . .is my flesh."*
JOHN 6:49–51 NLT

If you've never read all of the sixth chapter of John's Gospel, I encourage you to take a peek. After Jesus feeds five-thousand people, He has a bit of a nutty conversation with some Jews in the crowd. These folks who'd just seen this amazing sign asked Jesus for a sign—*what?*—and then were sort of bragging about the miracle God performed by providing manna to their ancestors in the wilderness. It just got weird. And Jesus wants them to hear that He is giving them something more than calories and carbs: He's offering them *eternal life*.

*God, I confess I'm like those people Jesus fed.
I understand earthly bread that keeps me alive today,
but it's harder for me to grasp the good news of
eternal life! Thank You for providing the
real Bread of Life. Amen.*

IF YOU'RE WEARY, WALK THIS WAY

"Come to me, all you who are weary and burdened, and I will give you rest. Take my yoke upon you and learn from me, for I am gentle and humble in heart, and you will find rest for your souls. For my yoke is easy and my burden is light."
MATTHEW 11:28–30

Have you ever thought about who Jesus might approach or spend time with in the halls of your high school? (Homeschooled friend, you've seen movies; you know how it goes.) Because Jesus is clear that He's come for the sick, the marginalized, and the weary, I can begin to imagine it. I think he'd find the kid who tripped and fell on his face in gym class. I suspect he'd find the girl who feels uncomfortable about the way her body appears to others. I think he'd find the young person who struggles with his or her English language skills. And I am certain that Jesus would find the one who is teased, bullied, weary, and burdened. If you're weary and burdened, Jesus came for you.

Jesus, I am grateful that You didn't just come for the healthy, the strong, and the popular! You came for me. Teach me to share Your yoke and find rest for my soul. Amen.

A FATHER WHO GIVES GOOD GIFTS

"Which of you, if your son asks for bread, will give him a stone?
Or if he asks for a fish, will give him a snake? If you, then, though you
are evil, know how to give good gifts to your children, how much more
will your Father in heaven give good gifts to those who ask him!"
MATTHEW 7:9–11

As infants, when we're wet, hungry, tired, or in pain, we learn whether there is a reliable "other" who will answer our cries. Ideally, there is! But sometimes, especially as we get older, our caregivers aren't able to meet all of our physical, emotional, and spiritual needs—for all kinds of reasons. So it's natural for us to believe that God is like the ill-equipped parents we've known. But Jesus, who assumes that parents want to do right by their children, goes on to say that God gives us *good gifts*. If you struggle with trusting God as a good parent, invite God to speak to your heart about it.

Father, I know that You are like no other. Teach my
heart that You are reliable, that You can be
trusted, and that You delight in meeting
my needs. I put my trust in You. Amen.

THE ONE WHO IS AN EVER-PRESENT HELP

God is our refuge and strength, an ever-present help in trouble.
Therefore we will not fear, though the earth give way and the
mountains fall into the heart of the sea, though its waters roar
and foam and the mountains quake with their surging.
PSALM 46:1-3

If you know and love God, you've no doubt been told that you can trust God in any circumstance, right? And specifically, you can trust God when things are difficult. Maybe you're willing to believe things will get better after you fail a test. Or you can sort of trust that God will comfort you when you and your boyfriend break up. But the psalmist kind of tops most of the challenges we face when he says, in essence, "Even if the earth breaks in half, we won't be afraid." That's *big faith*, right?! Graciously, God isn't measuring our faith, or the challenges we face. Rather, we have the confidence that whatever we face—a failed test or a natural disaster—God is our refuge and strength.

Lord, I thank You that, throughout the generations,
You have proven yourself to be reliable. With the
confidence of the psalmist, I put my trust
in You today, in Jesus' name. Amen.

SINS FORGIVEN AND BODIES HEALED

"Which is easier: to say, 'Your sins are forgiven,' or to say, 'Get up and walk'? But I want you to know that the Son of Man has authority on earth to forgive sins." So he said to the paralyzed man, "Get up, take your mat and go home." Then the man got up and went home. When the crowd saw this, they were filled with awe; and they praised God, who had given such authority to man.
MATTHEW 9:5–8

When Jesus arrived in His hometown of Nazareth, some men brought a paralyzed man to Him. Jesus recognized the faith of these friends and said that the man's sins were forgiven. The bold move was wildly offensive to religious people who believed only God could forgive sin. Aware that this was how teachers of the Law thought, Jesus proved His authority by announcing to the man, "Get up, take your mat and go home." When they saw it, the crowd was filled with awe and praised God.

Lord Jesus, You are amazing. You forgive, and You heal our bodies from the sting of death, disease, and disability—sometimes today and sometimes on the final day. With that crowd, I praise You! Amen.

HE HAS BORNE WHAT WE COULD NOT BEAR

*Surely he took up our pain and bore our suffering, yet we considered
him punished by God, stricken by him, and afflicted. But he was
pierced for our transgressions, he was crushed for our iniquities;
the punishment that brought us peace was on him,
and by his wounds we are healed.*

ISAIAH 53:4–5

As a young adult I was given the opportunity to face some of the bumps
and bruises that I'd endured during childhood. And as I offered those
hurts to God, He assured me that He loved me. But I had a hard time
receiving the love and healing God was offering me. But in that moment,
I saw, with the eyes of my heart, a picture of Jesus hanging on the cross.
And although I'd been a Christian for years, I suddenly "got it" in a new
way for the first time. *He loved me so much*, I realized, *that He gave His
life for mine.* As I held that in my heart, God was faithful to heal the
hurts from my past.

*God, You are a faithful redeemer and healer.
Thank You that You have taken my sins
upon You, and thank You that by Your
wounds mine are healed. Amen.*

KEEP YOUR EYES ON THE PRIZE

To You I lift up my eyes, O You who are enthroned in the heavens!
Behold, as the eyes of servants look to the hand of their master,
as the eyes of a maid to the hand of her mistress, so our eyes
look to the LORD our God, until He is gracious to us.
PSALM 123:1–2 NASB

During the civil rights movement in the United States in the 1950s and 1960s, those in the struggle sang Gospel songs and other freedom songs for encouragement. The lyrics from one exhort, "Keep your eye on the prize and hold on, hold on." The song resonates with echoes from Psalm 123. The psalmist reminds the worshipper that the eyes of servants are fixed on their masters. The eyes of a maid are fixed on the hand of her mistress. And the eyes of those who trust the Lord are fixed on Him. Today you are being invited to keep your eyes fixed on God, who is gracious to you.

Lord, I set my gaze on You. Equip me to ignore
the many interferences that would distract me
from staying focused on You. Today,
my eyes are fixed on You. Amen.

IF YOU DO WHAT IS RIGHT. . .

*"If you will give earnest heed to the voice of the LORD your God,
and do what is right in His sight, and give ear to His commandments,
and keep all His statutes, I will put none of the diseases on you which
I have put on the Egyptians; for I, the LORD, am your healer."*
EXODUS 15:26 NASB

When God's people were enslaved in Egypt, the Lord sent Moses to be their deliverer. And part of God's rescue plan was a series of plagues that afflicted the Egyptians. The big finale, though, was the parting of the Red Sea. When Moses stretched out his hand over the sea, the waters parted and the Hebrew people passed through on dry ground. But when Pharaoh's soldiers followed them, the waters swept their pursuers into the sea. Safe on the other side, God instructed His people to continue to heed His voice and respond in obedience to Him, so that they would flourish. God's Word reminds us that sometimes we participate with God in our own redemption and healing.

*Lord, You are a mighty deliverer. And I also hear You
inviting me to heed Your Word and walk in Your ways.
So I commit myself to partner with You! Amen.*

GOD MADE US FIERCE

For God did not give us a spirit of timidity (of cowardice, of craven and cringing and fawning fear), but [He has given us a spirit] of power and of love and of calm and well-balanced mind and discipline and self-control.

2 TIMOTHY 1:7 AMPC

One of the words used to describe Christians that makes some of us cringe is *nice*. Technically, I suppose there are worse words. I get that. But it just kind of smacks of being bland and flavorless and weak. In one of Paul's little letters to young Timothy, he reminds him that he was not made for "niceness." Instead, God gives believers a spirit of power, and love, and self-control. That means that in the face of conflict, hate, chaos, and confusion, Christian believers are infused by God with a mighty spirit of power.

God, I do believe that You made me to be fierce! Fill me with Your Spirit so that I might live a life of love and power and discipline that honors You. Amen.

WHAT YOU DID FOR THEM, YOU DID FOR ME

"Then the righteous will answer him, 'Lord, when did we see you
hungry and feed you, or thirsty and give you something to drink?
When did we see you a stranger and invite you in, or needing clothes
and clothe you? When did we see you sick or in prison and go to visit
you?' The King will reply, 'Truly I tell you, whatever you did for one
of the least of these brothers and sisters of mine, you did for me.' "
MATTHEW 25:37–40

Have you ever pulled up at a streetlight beside someone holding a sign asking for money? Christians respond in all different ways to folks in need. One might share food. Another might offer money. And another might introduce himself. Another might drive right past. In a story Jesus told, He said that the way we treat these—the hungry, the thirsty, the stranger, the naked, the sick, the imprisoned—is the way we treat Him! The next time you have the opportunity, pray, asking God how you should treat Jesus.

Lord, open my eyes to see Your face in the faces
of those in need. And teach me to be Your faithful
servant by meeting the needs of those
who are vulnerable. Amen.

COME, LET US BOW DOWN

Come, let us bow down in worship, let us kneel before the LORD
our Maker; for he is our God and we are the people
of his pasture, the flock under his care.

PSALM 95:6-7

Have you ever noticed how our bodies can be a reflection of what's inside of us? If we're rocking out to a praise song on Sunday morning, our arms might be outstretched toward the sky. If we're discouraged, our shoulders might be slumped and our eyes turned downward. If we're feeling really proud, we might stand a little taller with our head in the air. And when we go before the Lord, the psalmist invites us to bow down. Although we don't always *have* to kneel when we pray, it is a way of showing our humility in the presence of a mighty God. Our posture shows that we are willing to submit to God's will.

God, You are my Maker and my God! I praise You.
And I humble myself before You as a sign that
You are God and I am not. Be glorified
through my life today. Amen.

YOU ARE IN ME, AND I AM IN YOU

"On that day you will realize that I am in my Father, and you are in me, and I am in you. Whoever has my commands and keeps them is the one who loves me. The one who loves me will be loved by my Father, and I too will love them and show myself to them."

JOHN 14:20-21

Have you ever seen those little Russian nesting dolls? They're like hollow wooden eggs, carved out and painted in bright, beautiful colors. If you open up the largest doll, a smaller one will be inside. And if you open up that one, you'll find one that's smaller still. Each doll dwells *within* another. As Jesus is completing His earthly ministry, He's coaching His disciples about how to live in His absence. And the nesting situation He describes is that He's in His Father, and we are in Him. And if you open up the doll once more, we discover that Jesus is also *in us!* Jesus gives us this beautiful picture of not only being nestled inside the heart of the Father and the Son, but also filled with Jesus from the inside out.

Jesus, thank You for the security I have to dwell in You and know that You dwell in me. Because of Your promise, I am never alone. Amen.

155

YOU ARE A ROYAL PRIESTHOOD

*But you are a chosen people, a royal priesthood, a holy nation,
God's special possession, that you may declare the praises of him
who called you out of darkness into his wonderful light. Once you
were not a people, but now you are the people of God; once you
had not received mercy, but now you have received mercy.*

1 PETER 2:9–10

If you're not up to speed on your Church history, you might not realize
that until the sixteenth century, there was just one Church. In fact the
word *catholic*, originally from a Greek word, means "universal." But
during that period some Christians were upset about abuses that were
happening in the Church, creating barriers for laypeople to have access
to Jesus. And in this little New Testament epistle, they read that Peter
calls the early Christians "a royal priesthood." Essentially that means
that every person who has been saved by Jesus both has access to God
and is called to be a minister of God's grace to others. That includes you!

*God, I thank You for choosing me, saving me,
and making me Your own. Teach me to
declare Your praises! Amen.*

WISDOM IS FOUND ON THE LIPS OF THE WISE

Wisdom is found on the lips of the discerning, but a rod is for the back of one who has no sense. The wise store up knowledge, but the mouth of a fool invites ruin.

PROVERBS 10:13-14

Throughout Proverbs and other wisdom literature in the Old Testament, scripture extols the virtue of wisdom over foolishness. And in many of the examples we read in the Bible, a person's character is revealed by their tongue. The foolish cause harm with their words; the wise speak truth that brings life. What is unleashed when you speak? Words that bring death or ones that bring life? If the filter between your brain and your mouth isn't an effective one—meaning you blurt thoughtless words or spew angry ones—ask God to help you keep a rein on your tongue. It is a prayer God loves to answer.

Lord, I confess that sometimes my mouth gets away with me. Forgive me. Teach me this day how to honor You every time I open my mouth. Amen.

FROM NOW ON. . .

*For he and all his companions were astonished at the catch of fish
they had taken, and so were James and John, the sons of Zebedee,
Simon's partners. Then Jesus said to Simon, "Don't be afraid;
from now on you will fish for people." So they pulled their
boats up on shore, left everything and followed him.*

LUKE 5:9–11

The very first disciples Jesus called were two pairs of brothers He met
down at the lake. The four of them were fishermen. After a fruitless day
of pulling up empty nets, Jesus showed these guys where to cast their
nets, and they pulled in a huge haul! Amazed, they were captivated by the
person of Jesus. And when He called them to cast their nets for *people*
instead of fish, their response was radical. They left the family business
behind and followed Him! Jesus' call is one that radically changes the
lives of those who respond to His voice.

*Jesus, I believe that like You called four fishermen,
You are also calling me to follow You in radical ways.
Open my ears to hear Your voice, and give me
courage to respond in obedience! Amen.*

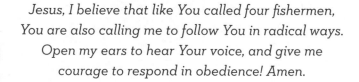

I BELIEVE

Jesus said, "If? There are no 'ifs' among believers.
Anything can happen." . . . The father cried,
"Then I believe. Help me with my doubts!"
MARK 9:23–24 MSG

When Jesus was speaking to a crowd, a father came to Him asking for help for his son. The boy was possessed by a demon and would be violently thrown to the ground. Jesus' disciples hadn't been able to heal the boy, but this dad still had hope that *maybe* Jesus could heal him, asking, "if" He could do anything. When Jesus queried to see if the man had faith, the dad cried out, "Then I believe. Help me with my doubts." Isn't that a beautiful way to name the way we believe God with our limited human capacity? Other translations say, "I believe; help my unbelief." The father's cry is a beautiful prayer we can offer to God!

God, I believe; help my unbelief. I do believe that You
can do all things, and I put my trust in You. You
are a mighty healer and redeemer. Amen.

SHE FELT IN HER BODY THAT SHE WAS HEALED

*Immediately her flow of blood was dried up at the source,
and [suddenly] she felt in her body that she was healed. . . .
And Jesus, recognizing in Himself that the power proceeding
from Him had gone forth, turned around immediately
in the crowd and said, "Who touched My clothes?"*
MARK 5:29–30 AMPC

In Mark's Gospel, he tells the story of Jesus' unusual interaction with a woman who'd been bleeding for twelve years. (Can you imagine having your period for twelve days, let alone twelve years?!) She'd been to a series of doctors looking for help, but they'd just taken her money and left her worse off than before. Because she was bleeding, she knew she shouldn't touch Jesus, but something in her told her to do it. When she did, two things happened: Jesus felt power leave His body, and she felt her body experience healing. Her story is a reminder that there is *nothing* we can't bring to Jesus.

*Jesus, I thank You that You are a powerful healer.
And I thank You that I can bring anything I'm facing to
You, knowing that You are a worker of miracles. Amen.*

THE ONE WHO IS SLOW TO BECOME ANGRY

"You are a God of forgiveness, gracious and merciful, slow to become angry, and rich in unfailing love. You did not abandon them."
NEHEMIAH 9:17 NLT

Do you ever feel like you're always asking God to forgive the same old sins? When you pause to confess to God, does it sound like the same old words are looping on repeat? If so, you're not alone. And when we do begin to bring the same old sins to God, the enemy can start to hiss lies in our ears: "You're not really saved. You're not really forgiven. You're not really loved." But the scriptures paint a picture of a God who is altogether gracious and merciful. We worship a God who is not only slow to become angry, but who loves to forgive. Beloved, know that God is rich in unfailing love and welcomes every one of your prayers.

God, I thank You that forgiveness does not depend on me and does depend on You! You are gracious, merciful, forgiving, and rich in unfailing love. I praise You! Amen.

WHY SARAH LAUGHED

The LORD said to Abraham, "Why did Sarah laugh? Why did she say, 'Can an old woman like me have a baby?' Is anything too hard for the LORD? I will return about this time next year, and Sarah will have a son."
GENESIS 18:13–14 NLT

Did you know that Abraham's wife, Sarah, conceived a child when she was ninety years old? That just *doesn't* happen. Although menopause unfolds differently for every woman, most women's bodies are finished producing eggs not long after they're fifty. So we're pretty much talking about someone the age of your grandmother or great-grandmother giving birth! And do you know what Sarah's reaction was when the Lord announced that this was going to happen? She laughed! She was probably trying to catch her breath when she asked, "God, can an old woman like me have a baby?" But nothing—the scripture assures us—is too hard for the Lord. While conception is most likely not on your list, what is the unlikely thing you're asking God to do for you?

God, just as You knew the heart of Sarah, You know the hopes and dreams I hold in my heart. And I offer You the most unlikely possibilities, believing that You can do anything. Amen.

MY THOUGHTS ARE NOT YOUR THOUGHTS. . .

"For My thoughts are not your thoughts, nor are your ways
My ways," declares the LORD. "For as the heavens are higher
than the earth, so are My ways higher than your ways
and My thoughts than your thoughts."
ISAIAH 55:8–9 NASB

Have you ever thought about how you might handle things if you were in charge of the world? Sometimes it's tempting to believe that, given the chance, we could manage things a little bit better than the One who's in charge right now. But the fact is that when we look at situations, we see them only with our limited human imagination. We don't have the capacity to see what God sees, hear what God hears, or think the thoughts God thinks. As a result, we're sometimes left scratching our heads. But Isaiah reminds us that because God's ways are higher than our ways, we can trust even what we can't understand.

Lord, I confess that Your thoughts are higher than
my thoughts and Your ways higher than my ways.
Teach me to trust You more deeply. Amen.

163

THEY WILL NEVER FOLLOW A STRANGER

*"When he has brought out all his own, he goes on ahead of them,
and his sheep follow him because they know his voice. But they
will never follow a stranger; in fact, they will run away from
him because they do not recognize a stranger's voice."*
JOHN 10:4–5

Researchers recently discovered that although it takes young children more than five minutes to wake up to a standard smoke detector alarm, they wake up in just four seconds when they hear the sound of their mothers' voices! So now parents who purchase smart smoke detectors can program a voice message telling their child, by name, to get out of bed and leave the room. Children's natural resonance with a voice they trust is what Jesus is describing when He says that the sheep follow the voice of the shepherd and run from the voice of a stranger. What are the ways that you hear and discern the voice of the Shepherd who is good?

*Jesus, I thank You that You've made yourself known
as a Good Shepherd. Help me stay alert to the
sound of Your voice and follow after You. Amen.*

BECAUSE I LOVE YOU

"For I am the LORD your God, the Holy One of Israel, your Savior;
I give Egypt for your ransom, Cush and Seba in your stead. Since you
are precious and honored in my sight, and because I love you,
I will give people in exchange for you, nations in exchange for
your life. Do not be afraid, for I am with you; I will bring
your children from the east and gather you from the west."
ISAIAH 43:3-5

You know how your heart feels warm when a parent says that he or she loves you? Because we were made to give and receive love, we are wired to be in loving relationships with others. During the time Isaiah lived, God's people had been scattered in exile, and God is comforting them with the assurance of His love. God promises to do anything to save them, saying, "You are precious and honored in my sight, and because I love you. . ." Listen this week for God's voice confirming His love for you.

Lord, thank You for the assurance in Your Word that
You are with us and for us. Open the ears of my
heart so that I can hear Your words of love. Amen.

A MEDIATOR WHO GETS IT

Therefore, since we have a great high priest who has ascended into heaven, Jesus the Son of God, let us hold firmly to the faith we profess. For we do not have a high priest who is unable to empathize with our weaknesses, but we have one who has been tempted in every way, just as we are—yet he did not sin.

HEBREWS 4:14-15

Imagine that a man who was wrongly imprisoned was released and decided to study and practice law. If you were a person who was wrongly imprisoned, wouldn't you want this attorney to advocate for you? You'd want him to represent you because he would understand what your life is like. God's Word assures us that our Advocate is able to empathize with our weaknesses. Because Jesus, who's now ascended into heaven, walked the earth in human flesh like ours, He understands intimately the temptations we face. Because He was tempted too, He is our faithful mediator.

Jesus, I thank You that You know exactly what it's like to be human! When You present my case before the Father, You understand my temptations. I praise You for being my faithful priest. Amen.

THINK ON WHAT IS GOOD

Finally, brothers and sisters, whatever is true, whatever is noble, whatever is right, whatever is pure, whatever is lovely, whatever is admirable—if anything is excellent or praiseworthy—think about such things. Whatever you have learned or received or heard from me, or seen in me—put it into practice. And the God of peace will be with you.

PHILIPPIANS 4:8-9

Would you say that what's in our minds can be sinful, or is it just what we do with our actions? God's Word reminds us that what we think about, what we pour into our brains, matters. That includes the movies we watch, the lyrics we listen to, the books we read, and even the friends with whom we hang out! Because those thoughts shape the way we'll behave. They *form* us. And that's why Paul reminds his brothers and sisters in the church in Philippi to choose to think on that which is excellent or praiseworthy. Are there ways God is calling you to adjust your thinking?

Lord, You know every thought I have before I have it. Because I long to please You, help me recognize and banish thoughts that don't glorify You, and choose instead to think on what is true, noble, right, pure, lovely, admirable, excellent, and praiseworthy. Amen.

CHILDREN, OBEY YOUR PARENTS

Children, obey your parents in the Lord, for this is right. "Honor your father and mother"—which is the first commandment with a promise— "so that it may go well with you and that you may enjoy long life on the earth." Fathers, do not exasperate your children; instead, bring them up in the training and instruction of the Lord.

EPHESIANS 6:1–4

When our parents give us rides to friends' homes, buy us the clothes we want, encourage us to invite friends over for dinner, and tell us they love us, it's not a big chore to obey them. But what about the times when they're not at their best? Are we supposed to obey them then? One of the Ten Commandments says we are! Even when we disagree with a decision our folks have made, we're still called to honor them. When is it hardest for you to honor your parents? How is God helping you in those moments?

Lord, thank You that You've placed me in a family— even an imperfect one! Help me to respect and honor my parents in a way that glorifies You. Amen.

THE WAY TO PRAY

*"And when you pray, do not be like the hypocrites, for they love to
pray standing in the synagogues and on the street corners to be seen
by others. Truly I tell you, they have received their reward in full.
But when you pray, go into your room, close the door and
pray to your Father, who is unseen. Then your Father,
who sees what is done in secret, will reward you."*
MATTHEW 6:5–6

When Jesus taught His disciples how to pray, He used the religious
folks in their community as a *counterexample*! Those folks were praying
in a way that displeased God, making a big show of doing it in public
where they could be seen and heard. They used lots of words, as if more
words would somehow be more persuasive to the Almighty! And Jesus
prescribed the exact opposite for those who want to be rewarded by
God: find a place where no one can see you and be efficient with your
words! Is there a "secret place" in your home where you can speak
privately to God?

*God, I thank You for this assurance from Jesus that
You see what is done in secret. Thank You that You are
faithful to meet me in the secret place. Amen.*

GOD NEVER FORGETS

"Yet I will remember the covenant I made with you in the days of your youth, and I will establish an everlasting covenant with you."
EZEKIEL 16:60

Ezekiel tells a compelling story of God walking past an abandoned newborn infant, flailing in her own blood. Recognizing her need, God bathes and dresses her, adorning her with the finest jewelry, and enters into a covenant with her. And when she gets older and becomes a queen, the word of her beauty spreads throughout the nations. But then she is unfaithful to her groom. Although God's beloved one breaks the covenant, God remains faithful to her. This is our story as well: God saved us; we continued to sin; God remained, and remains, faithful. Every day this is our story! And every day God remembers the covenant He made with us and remains faithful.

Lord, thank You that Yours is an everlasting covenant.
Despite my sin, You keep Your word. And thank You
that, no matter what I do, You remain faithful. Amen.

TREASURE IN CLAY JARS

But we have this treasure in jars of clay to show that this all-surpassing power is from God and not from us. We are hard pressed on every side, but not crushed; perplexed, but not in despair; persecuted, but not abandoned; struck down, but not destroyed.

2 CORINTHIANS 4:7-9

If I were giving someone a treasure, I'm pretty sure I know how I'd do it. I'd begin by hiring an armored truck with big strong guards. They would deliver my treasure to the recipient's home or place of business where it would be locked away in a secure safe. But this is not what God has done with His treasure—the Gospel that gives life to the world—at all! Instead, God has entrusted it to us, whom He calls "clay jars." Isn't that a crazy choice? God pours out His all-surpassing power into cracked pots like us. And as a result, God is the One who is glorified as the source of the treasure, and not us.

Father, it really doesn't make sense that You'd choose to use a fragile vessel like me, but thank You for pouring Your grace, Your life, and Your power into me. Teach me to be a faithful steward. Amen.

THIS IS WHY I KNEEL BEFORE THE FATHER

For this reason I kneel before the Father, from whom every family in heaven and on earth derives its name. I pray that out of his glorious riches he may strengthen you with power through his Spirit in your inner being, so that Christ may dwell in your hearts through faith. And I pray that you, being rooted and established in love, may have power, together with all the Lord's holy people, to grasp how wide and long and high and deep is the love of Christ, and to know this love that surpasses knowledge—that you may be filled to the measure of all the fullness of God.

EPHESIANS 3:14-19

Did someone in your family teach you to pray? Maybe your mom repeated a prayer with you at bedtime. Or maybe your grandmother had you kneel beside your bed, clasp your hands, and bow your head while she prayed. As we listen in on Paul's prayer for the believers in Ephesus, his heart is that followers of Jesus would understand the seismic proportions of His love for them! Isn't it a beautiful prayer? Today, pray it for someone you love.

Father, fill the ones I love with the awareness of Your big, big love for them. Amen.

CLOTHE YOURSELVES WITH THESE

Therefore, as God's chosen people, holy and dearly loved,
clothe yourselves with compassion, kindness, humility, gentleness and
patience. Bear with each other and forgive one another if any of
you has a grievance against someone. Forgive as the Lord
forgave you. And over all these virtues put on love,
which binds them all together in perfect unity.
COLOSSIANS 3:12-14

Are you the kind of girl who lays out your clothes for school the night before, or do you race around in the morning grabbing whatever is clean? Whichever way you roll, the outfit you wear—warm and cozy on a cold day or light and breezy on a warm one—prepares you for the day. And that's what Paul is describing when he tells the Colossians how to clothe themselves. No, he's not suggesting shorts or jeans. He's teaching believers to clothe themselves with a holy wardrobe: compassion, kindness, humility, gentleness, and patience. He also advises practicing forgiveness and, for outerwear, putting love on over them all.

Lord, I can see how donning the wardrobe You
provide equips me to live well! Today I choose
compassion, kindness, humility, gentleness,
patience, forgiveness, and love. Amen.

I WILL NOT LEAVE YOU

"I am with you, and I will protect you wherever you go. One day I will bring you back to this land. I will not leave you until I have finished giving you everything I have promised you." Then Jacob awoke from his sleep and said, "Surely the LORD is in this place, and I wasn't even aware of it!"

GENESIS 28:15–16 NLT

After stopping to sleep in the middle of a journey, God gave Jacob a holy dream. In it, he saw angels ascending and descending a staircase between Earth and heaven. After identifying Himself as the God of his grandfather and father, the Lord promised to give the land where he slept to Jacob and his descendants, assuring him that the whole earth would be blessed by them. Concluding, God assured Jacob that He'd stay with him until it was accomplished. For the rest of his life, Jacob could count on that promise. Is there a promise of God you've received, through scripture or prayer, for which you are trusting God?

Lord, although I can't always discern the twists and turns in my journey with You, I trust in Your Word and in Your promises. Today, I believe that You will do what You've said You will do. Amen.

THIS IS HOW GOD SHOWED HIS LOVE

This is how God showed his love among us: He sent his one and only Son into the world that we might live through him.

1 JOHN 4:9

I'll bet there are days when God's love for you seems as close and real as your own skin. But other days, God's love is harder to *feel*. You might still believe it in your head, and even in your heart, but it's harder to feel it in your bones. Have you had days like that? When you do, return to this beautiful assurance from 1 John 4. He assures us that we can be assured of God's love in our deep places because He sent His Son Jesus into the world for us. Though some of us take that for granted, it is a huge gift. Jesus first gave up His heavenly privileges and then gave up His life on earth out of His big love for you.

Father, I confess that I don't always feel the reality of Your love. But in the life of Jesus, I have evidence of the big love You have for me. Thank You for that gift. Amen.

DON'T DECEIVE YOURSELVES

*Do not merely listen to the word, and so deceive yourselves. Do what
it says. Anyone who listens to the word but does not do what it says
is like someone who looks at his face in a mirror and, after looking at
himself, goes away and immediately forgets what he looks like.
But whoever looks intently into the perfect law that gives freedom,
and continues in it—not forgetting what they have heard,
but doing it—they will be blessed in what they do.*

JAMES 1:22–25

Did you know there are *risks* to being a Christian who walks with God
and listens to His Word? One of those risks, that we don't always talk
about, is the risk of hearing God's Word and not *doing* it. Okay, it may
not feel as perilous as facing a grizzly bear, but it is the spiritual equiv-
alent of facing a bear! Our hearts are at risk when we receive the Word
but then forget it, failing to respond in obedience to what we've learned.
Today, purpose to put into action what God has shown you.

*Lord, send Your Spirit to nudge my heart, mind,
and body to action. Equip me to be the person who
acts on what I discover in Your Word. Amen.*

YOU ARE SURROUNDED BY THE LORD'S UNFAILING LOVE

Many are the woes of the wicked, but the LORD's unfailing love
surrounds the one who trusts in him. Rejoice in the LORD and be
glad, you righteous; sing, all you who are upright in heart!

PSALM 32:10–11

In Psalm 32 the writer names the *goodness* of being surrounded by God's unfailing love. So I want you to ask God to show you how you are surrounded by His unfailing love for you. Maybe God will give you a glimpse of your earliest days, in your mother's womb, surrounded by her love for you. Or maybe you'll see yourself cuddled up in your favorite blankie as a little girl. Or maybe you'll imagine being circled up at the family dinner table, at Thanksgiving or Christmas, surrounded by love. Or maybe you'll imagine all of your friends encircling you with their love. These are just pictures, symbolizing a love that does not fail. Beloved, know that in every moment you are surrounded by God's unfailing love for you.

God, thank You for a love that does not fail. Today I
believe the promise I receive from Your Word that I
am embraced by Your unfailing love. Amen.

SAVED FROM THE STORM

Then he got into the boat and his disciples followed him. Suddenly a furious storm came up on the lake, so that the waves swept over the boat. But Jesus was sleeping. The disciples went and woke him, saying, "Lord, save us! We're going to drown!" He replied, "You of little faith, why are you so afraid?" Then he got up and rebuked the winds and the waves, and it was completely calm.

MATTHEW 8:23–26

In the first century—and even today!—those who toil for a living outdoors and depend on the sea for transportation are vulnerable to the elements. When Jesus' friends were in a boat with Him and a storm arose, they felt more than vulnerable. They were terrified! In fact, these seasoned sailors believed they would die. But when they turned to Jesus for help, He calmed the storm. You may not face lightning, winds, and waves, but I suspect that there are eruptions in your life that scare you. Know that you can entrust these to the One who loves you.

Jesus, I trust You with my life. And specifically, I offer to You the parts of my life that scare me. The ones I have no control over. You are Lord of all. Amen.

YOU WON'T BE DISAPPOINTED

"When you come looking for me, you'll find me. Yes, when you get serious about finding me and want it more than anything else, I'll make sure you won't be disappointed. . . . I'll turn things around for you."
JEREMIAH 29:13–14 MSG

Sometimes the assignments God gives are great ones: share good news with someone, visit an elderly neighbor, or invest in the life of a child. But other assignments are more difficult. That was true of Jeremiah. Sent by God to speak to a people in exile, Jeremiah wrote and sent a letter to those who were suffering in exile, delivering God's Word to them. And in the midst of terribly difficult circumstances, God promises to show up for these desperate ones. "I'll make sure you won't be disappointed," God assures them. "I'll turn things around for you." Can you hear God speaking these words of hope to your heart today?

Lord, You know the parts of my life where I am discouraged. Where it's hard to see what You're up to. But because I believe that You are a God who never leaves me or forsakes me, my eyes are open to see Your face! Amen.

I WILL NEVER TAKE AWAY MY LOVE

"But my love will never be taken away from him, as I took it away from Saul, whom I removed from before you. Your house and your kingdom will endure forever before me; your throne will be established forever."

2 SAMUEL 7:15–16

Before David ruled over the nation of Israel, a man named Saul had been Israel's king. But God wasn't pleased with Saul. After Saul died by falling on his own sword to avoid capture in battle, Samuel appointed David to succeed him. It was a really big deal that God called David His son. And God promised David that although He'd taken His love away from Saul, He would never remove His love from David. And we share in that promise today. Because of Jesus, because of His sacrifice that gives us a relationship with the Father, we have confidence that God's love can never be taken from us.

God, I thank You that Your love for me never fails.
Like David, You have called me Your own. Teach me,
this day, to honor You in all I do. Amen.

BE STRONG IN THE LORD

*Finally, be strong in the Lord and in his mighty power. Put on the full
armor of God, so that you can take your stand against the devil's
schemes. For our struggle is not against flesh and blood, but against
the rulers, against the authorities, against the powers of this dark
world and against the spiritual forces of evil in the heavenly realms.*

EPHESIANS 6:10-12

When I go roller skating on Saturday mornings, I walk about a mile to
a paved trail then put on my wrist guards, elbow pads, and knee pads.
Then I buckle the chin strap of my helmet under my chin. Daily God
invites us to put on the armor He provides for our protection. (Learn
more about it in Ephesians 6:13-17!) This isn't gear that protects us from
sprained wrists, but armor like a belt of truth and a shield of faith to
protect us from spiritual attacks. And when we wear it daily—maybe
even praying the armor "on" as we get dressed in the morning!—we are
protected by God.

*Lord, I thank You that You are my refuge and strong
defender. And when I face spiritual threats, I thank
You for the power of Your Holy Spirit that
keeps me safe. Amen.*

GOD REJOICES OVER YOU WITH JOY

The Lord your God is in the midst of you, a Mighty One, a Savior
[Who saves]! He will rejoice over you with joy; He will rest [in silent
satisfaction] and in His love He will be silent and make no mention
[of past sins, or even recall them]; He will exult over you with singing.
ZEPHANIAH 3:17 AMPC

Have you ever closed your eyes and tried to picture the face of Jesus'
Father? Okay, God doesn't have a physical face, but as one of three persons in the Trinity, God does relate to us, right? Some people see God
as an overly eager cop, who's always trying to catch us doing something
wrong. Others see God's face as looking like a harsh judge who's quick
to proclaim guilt and judgment. But the picture described in Zephaniah
gives us a glimpse of a very different face. This passage assures us that
God *rejoices* over us with *joy!* Can you see that face? It is a face that
says, *"You matter!"*

God, I confess that I sometimes believe You look
like the human faces I've known. Thank You for
this beautiful picture of Your gracious face
that exults over me with singing. Amen.

THIS IS THE DAY THE LORD HAS MADE

This is the day the LORD has made.
We will rejoice and be glad in it.
PSALM 118:24 NLT

Have you ever had one of those days when everything goes wrong? Maybe you misplaced your bus pass or car keys before school. Or you tripped on the stairs walking to gym class. Or maybe you got your period at the *worst* time. In those moments, it's easy to feel alone and like no one cares for you. But the psalmist announced that today—and yesterday, and also tomorrow—is a day that God has made. Nothing that happens to you escapes God's notice. Nothing you face is a surprise to God. That also means that there's nothing God won't help you get through. When you face challenges this week, know that God is with you and God is for you.

Faithful God, You know that I am not keen on rejoicing
in some of what I am facing. But I do believe that
You are Lord of all and You are my helper.
Today I open my eyes and ears to notice the
ways that You are with me and for me. Amen.

BECAUSE WE DON'T KNOW WHAT TO PRAY

*We don't know what God wants us to pray for. But the Holy Spirit
prays for us with groanings that cannot be expressed in words.
And the Father who knows all hearts knows what the Spirit is saying,
for the Spirit pleads for us believers in harmony with God's own will.*
ROMANS 8:26–27 NLT

Sometimes we know exactly what to pray for, because God's will has
been made plain in scripture. Other times, we wrestle to know the very
best way to pray. I'm thinking of a foster mom who was going to court
to find out whether the children she loved would be returned to their
families of origin. But because she couldn't see everything that God
saw, she realized that she didn't know what was best for the precious
children in her care. In moments like this, it's okay not to know. And we
have the confidence that when we tip our faces toward God, the Spirit
interprets the groanings of our hearts to the Father.

*God, You know what's on my heart right now.
And because I don't know what outcome to seek,
I invite Your Spirit to pray with me, and I trust
that You listen and You care. Amen.*

DO NOT BE AFRAID

*"Don't be afraid, for I am with you. Don't be discouraged, for I am
your God. I will strengthen you and help you. I will hold you up with
my victorious right hand. . . . For I hold you by your right hand—I,
the LORD your God. And I say to you, 'Don't be afraid.
I am here to help you. . . . I will help you.'"*

ISAIAH 41:10, 13–14 NLT

A long time ago there was a comedian named Bob Newhart who played
a therapist on television. And when people would come to him with their
fears, he would offer them just two words: "Stop it!" It's funny, because
that's not how people work, is it? Being told *not* to be afraid doesn't make
us less afraid. But when God exhorts us to not be afraid, God continues,
"For I am with you." God promises to take the sufferer by the hand and
to strengthen and help the one in need. This week, hear God's voice
assuring you, *"I am with you."*

*God, You know the fears in my heart, and I entrust
them to You. Let me see Your face and hear Your voice,
so that I might know You are with me. Amen.*

I'VE COME THAT THEY MAY HAVE LIFE

"I am the gate; whoever enters through me will be saved. They will come in and go out, and find pasture. The thief comes only to steal and kill and destroy; I have come that they may have life, and have it to the full. I am the good shepherd. The good shepherd lays down his life for the sheep."
JOHN 10:9–11

When Jesus was helping crowds understand who He is, He contrasted Himself with the one He calls "the thief." In other places in scripture the thief is called Satan, the enemy, and the deceiver. This guy, claims Jesus, comes only to steal and kill and destroy. In contrast, Jesus has come so that the sheep He loves can have abundant life. And in the holy mystery of faith, the Shepherd who is good gives His own life so that we might be able to live. And although we wrestle to understand it, we also find life when we love others with this self-sacrificial love.

Lord, You know that, unchecked, I am wired to serve myself. But I long to pattern my life after You! Guide me as I purpose to give my life for the sake of others. Amen.

AND THEN I UNDERSTOOD

But when I considered how to understand this, it was too great
an effort for me and too painful until I went into the
sanctuary of God; then I understood.
PSALM 73:16–17 AMPC

Sometimes we're faced with a situation in life that we simply cannot understand. Maybe our parents tell us they're considering getting a divorce. Maybe someone we love dies. Or maybe we don't understand why we're not receiving the good gifts we've begged God for! With our human understanding, we're not always equipped to understand God's ways. But graciously we have the privilege of approaching God with our concerns. Sometimes when we do, God gives us the answer. And other times when we question God, He grants our hearts the peace we're after, even if we don't completely understand.

God, there are some things in my life that are just too
painful for me to understand. And so I bring them
to You, seeking Your wisdom. Speak, Lord,
for Your servant is listening. Amen.

YOU ARE MY BELOVED

When all the people were being baptized, Jesus was baptized too.
And as he was praying, heaven was opened and the Holy Spirit
descended on him in bodily form like a dove. And a voice came from
heaven: "You are my Son, whom I love; with you I am well pleased."
LUKE 3:21–22

Have you ever thought about why Jesus was baptized the way that we're baptized to be cleansed from our sins? (I mean, He was sinless, right? If it ain't broke, don't fix it!) This baptism, though, was different than the ones John the Baptist had been performing, because God *claims* Jesus as His own. First, the Father identifies Jesus as His own Son. Then, He proclaims His love for Him. And, finally, He announces His delight in Jesus! And although this event specifically identified Jesus as the Messiah, we can also hear whispers of God's love for us as well. Today, listen for God calling you His daughter, proclaiming His love for you, and even delighting in you.

God, I thank You that—like Jesus!—I belong to You.
You have called me Your own and I am Yours.
Teach me to live as Your beloved
daughter today. Amen.

SCRIPTURE INDEX

DISCOVER MORE INSPIRATION FOR YOUR LIFE

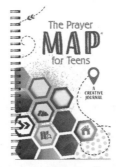

The Prayer Map for Teens

This purposeful prayer journal is a fun and creative way to more fully experience the power of prayer. Each page guides you to write out thoughts, ideas, and lists. . .which then creates a specific "map" for you to follow as you talk to God. Each map includes a spot to record the date, so you can look back on your prayers and see how God has worked in your life. *The Prayer Map* will not only encourage you to spend time talking with God about the things that matter most. . .it will also help you build a healthy spiritual habit of continual prayer for life!

Spiral Bound / 978-1-68322-556-0 / $7.99